Lewis

The Two Legged Fox

A True Tale of Victorian Gower

Rod Cooper

Subboscus

Published in 2008 by
Subboscus
The Lodge, Park Road, Penclawdd
Swansea, SA4 3FH
rcooper@yllety.f9.co.uk

A CIP catalogue record for this book is
available from the British Library.

ISBN 978-0-9534523-1-6

Printed and bound in Wales by
Dinefwr Press Ltd.
Rawlings Road, Llandybie
Carmarthenshire, SA18 3YD

Contents

Acknowledgements

Acknowledgements are far from a formality with this book. Without the pioneering work of Mrs Marilyn Jones in creating the database of the *Cambrian* newspaper which became the 'Cambrian Index', this book would never have been conceived; so my thanks must go first to her. For the happy discovery of the riches of Charles Morgan's diary, and for the free use which has kindly been allowed to use them, my very great thanks must go to Prys Morgan. I am also greatly indebted to him for the hours of free 'tutorials' I have had which have enormously expanded my view of local history. Many other people have been kind and helpful, especially the West Glamorgan Archive Service which is unfailingly efficient, prompt and courteous even when sorely tried. Mrs Pat Williams has been very helpful in respect of important details of Llanrhidian local history and some illustrative material. A fellow local historian from Dartmoor, Mr Trevor James of South Zeal, has also been most kind and helpful in giving me the use of some superb photographs of the prison.

My wife, Sue, has been extraordinarily patient and tolerant with my arcane researches but, above all, extremely supportive of the whole project of getting this text to print. At numberless venues she has run the slide projector or Powerpoint whilst I give talks about the 'Two Legged Fox'; her encouragement has resulted in this publication.

Finally, and posthumously, I must thank Christopher Batcock. He was not a neighbour, probably, to be wished on one's worst enemy. Had he read this book he might well have had the author by the throat! And yet the pleasure I have had in tracing his nefarious way through life has been enormous and, for this, I am truly grateful to him.

A Note on the Text

I have adopted a convention, when quoting from the *Cambrian* newspaper or from Charles Morgan's diaries, of using italics rather than inverted commas. It is hoped that this is helpful to the reader in making the text appear to 'flow' more easily on the page whilst at the same time indicating that the language used is not the author's but an authentic voice of the period.

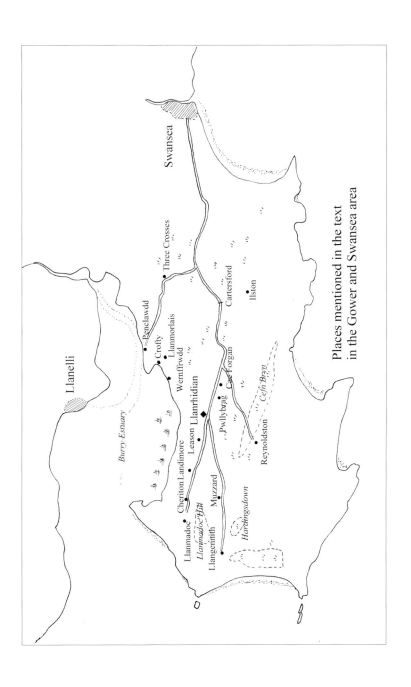

Places mentioned in the text
in the Gower and Swansea area

Swansea

Llanelli

Burry Estuary

Penclawdd

Three Crosses

Crofty

Llanmorlais

Wernffrwdd

Cartersford

Ilston

Cae Forgan

Cheriton Landimore

Leason Llanrhidian

Pwllybrag

Cefn Bryn

Reynoldston

Llanmadoc

Llanmadoc Hill

Muzzard

Llangennith

Hardingsdown

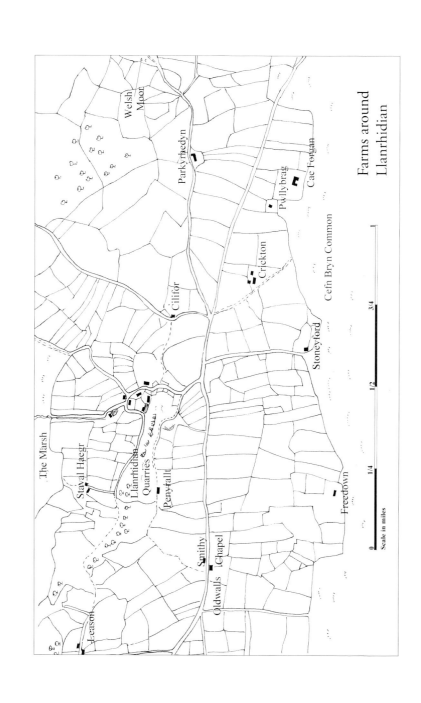

Farms around
Llanrhidian

Chapter One

Pwllybrag

It was probably better for them up there, away from the village. It was not a very big village, even now it is one of the smallest in Gower. At the time of the events in this story, Llanrhidian was a rather down-at-heel place. But the Batcocks were well out of it, up on the edge of the moors. Their home was called 'Pwllybrag', a Welsh name possibly translating as 'malt pool'. The moors up there were covered in little pools. It was right on the edge of the great sweep of moorland that sloped up to the top of Cefn Bryn, the long hill that runs like a backbone to much of Gower. The cottage ruins, today, speak of narrow confined lives within narrow confining walls. But in its day, Pwllybrag would have been seen as superior accommodation

Arthur's Stone – a nineteenth century print.

for the tough, working folk that lived in north Gower. There are records of Pwllybrag going back to the early 1700's when Philip Jenkinson lived there – the local courts complained of the state in which he kept the property.

Pwllybrag was just one of a number of little cottages-cum-farms that had sprung up over the centuries along the edge of the great moor of Cefn Bryn. Two fields to the east was the cottage of Cae Morgan. Four small fields to the west was Crickton, an old farm, and beyond this were more cottages at Stoneyford and Freedown – each with a couple of fields and some grazing on the common. All had many acres of empty moorland to the south, rising to the gentle crest of Cefn Bryn with just the great boulder of Arthur's Stone breaking the skyline as it had done for millennia before. To the north, they all had paths and lanes leading to the village of Llanrhidian just half a mile away.

We see Llanrhidian now as one of the gems of Gower – a steep lane descending to the marshlands of the Burry estuary past tidy cottages. A little green with standing stones, a beautiful medieval church and a picturesque mill at the bottom of the hill, an ancient village; it was probably more grim in times past. Mud churned up on the steep slope of Rocky Lane, every green spot blemished by traffic avoiding the worst ruts. Poor cottages with mouldy thatch. Old pictures suggest mangy ponies and thin cattle grazing in odd corners where a bit of grass survived. The church, throughout the 19th century, was constantly in need of repair and unroofed for some periods.

The population of this little village had been much the same for centuries with never more than about 800 people in the whole parish and less than half that in the village itself. The employment was all related to agriculture although the limestone quarries by the village engaged a few hands from

The village green and church at Llanrhidian.

time to time. There were two mills, 'Higher' and 'Lower', just to the west of the church which lay close to the centre of the village. Virtually every household, including the mills, was engaged in farming; most villagers still had a strip or two in the fields surrounding the village – a hangover from the communal farming of the medieval period. Most villagers had animals, especially sheep, grazing on the common of the marsh. So every household bore the marks of agricultural practice; it was, in effect, a village of small farms. Any growth in the village numbers was readily absorbed by the burgeoning industrialism of Swansea, just ten miles to the east. Even nearer to hand, the mines of Wernffrwd and Llanmorlais offered regular wages to those with a mind to walk the three miles there each day. Just a mile further was Penclawdd, a small port with copper works, coal mines and fishing. Since the Civil War, there had been growth in the mining industry around these villages – slow at first but, in the 18th century, vigorous and entrepreneurial. By 1800, however, and in the early decades of the 19th century, these heavy industries were struggling and Penclawdd fell on hard times.

Somehow, this onset of a new age did not seem to affect Pwllybrag. Like many other cottages along the moor's edge, it was probably built about 1700. It was a simple affair of low-ceilinged rooms either side of a central doorway and even lower rooms upstairs. The first records tell us of Philip Jenkinson living there in 1711 – 'we present', the leet court records say, 'Philip Jenkinson for not repairing his house at Pollybrage'. The following year he was presented for not keeping in repair the hedge at Cae Howell (the field adjoining Cae Morgan), nor his stable 'at Polthybrage' – it seems that Philip Jenkinson was not a tidy man. Old age may have been the reason; in 1714 'Philip Jenkin' is recorded by the court as dead and David Long in his

Pwllybrag as it looks today.

place. For a number of reasons we may assume that Philip Jenkin was indeed Philip Jenkinson – no 'Jenkinsons' are recorded in the registers and we know that the Longs were the next occupants of Pwllybrag.

So David Long moved into Pwllybrag and the Long family remained there for over a hundred years. By the 19th century, the Longs of Pwllybrag must have seemed as fixed a part of the parish as Arthur's Stone up on the hill above. About 1740 we find a David and Mary Long ensconced at Pwllybrag with children born from 1740 to at least 1748. There appears to have been a Martha, two (possibly three) Marys and an Elizabeth and one male heir – David. At one time in the 18th century there were at least five David Longs living concurrently in the parish and it is difficult to disentangle them in the registers and particularly difficult to ascertain dates of death for these people. However, we can be reasonably confident that the David Long recorded subsequently at Pwllybrag was the same as the one born to David and Mary in 1748. A survey carried

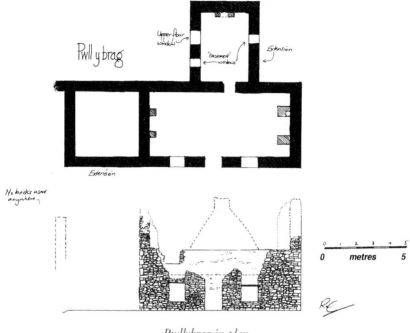

Pwllybrag in plan.

out by Gabriel Powell for the Duke of Beaufort in 1765 shows a David Long at Crickton, the neighbouring farm to the west and at Cae Morgan to the east. There was even a David Long at Parkyrhedin farm just a quarter of a mile to the north.

The parish registers record David Longs getting married in 1763, 1769, 1770, 1783 and 1787; the David Long we are interested in appears to have been one of these. On the 28th February, 1770, David married Mary Hancorne in Llanrhidian parish church. Because of the plethora of David Longs, 3 of whom married a Mary, it continues to be difficult to be certain of the offspring of this marriage but it seems likely that Griffith was born to the family in 1788, Maria in 1789 and Samuel

Hancorne in 1791. Both Maria and Samuel were living at Pwllybrag 20 years later when Maria married Robert Batcock, a local carpenter and general 'odd job' man. Maria and Robert lived at Pwllybrag together with her parents and brother. In 1815, a boy was born at Pwllybrag, but not to the newly-wed couple. The boy was Samuel's, and the mother was a Deborah Davies. This was after Maria had started her own family, so we can see that the house was beginning to get a little crowded.

Compared with the Long dynasty, Maria's husband Robert had a slightly less auspicious genealogy. Robert was a Llan-rhidian man and Batcocks had lived in the parish for as long as records exist. But the Longs were a more pervasive group in the parish whilst the Batcock genealogy seems fragmentary and difficult to piece together. Robert was born in 1782. His parents may have been Robert and Elinor (Harry) who married in 1774. There were one or two other Batcocks in the village but their origins are at least as vague. Being a relatively unusual name, particularly with the 't' spelling ('Badcock' is a more common name), we may assume that they all recognised some family connection. They were not the powerful family group that the Longs were, however, and it may be that Robert was slightly disadvantaged from the outset of his marriage to Maria.

It was a stirring time to live; never had the 'rights of man' been so boldly set forth. The French Revolution and Maria Long's birth coincided. Although the air of egalitarianism was abroad, it was discouraged at home and seen as part of a gen-erally unsettling political movement disadvantageous to the interests of the wealthy and established of Britain and threaten-ing to her wider international interests. Whatever local people thought of either side of the argument, this was no 'cap doffing' part of the world, nor were working men so tied to their 'super-iors' as in other parts of Britain. Opportunities in industry close at hand meant that farmers and landowners had less control over their rural workforce who, on occasions, had to be cajoled into work. If pay was poor or work over-demanding, labourers knew that other employment opportunities existed within a few miles that might offer a better quality of life. Even small-holders such as David Long and his successor Robert Batcock could feel they were, to some extent, 'their own man' as Welshmen traditionally have done.

This freedom of spirit, however, did not free them from the vicissitudes and realities of the times. The conclusion of the Napoleonic Wars took some of the drive out of the economy; both industry and agriculture felt the effects. Down in Pen-clawdd the copper works were in trouble and matters were not helped by the fact that the best seams of local coal had run out. For paltry cargoes, small vessels would not venture up the difficult estuary so docks, mines and works all lay idle. Although protected by the Corn Laws, agriculture was also experiencing difficulties. The year 1816, for example, seemed to be a year with no summer, cold and wet from start to finish. Hands were laid off for lack of harvest. The following year was quite the reverse – blazing hot with dreadful storms. Another harvest ruined and real distress in the village. The high price of corn ensured that farmers survived but poor folk suffered. People began to leave the land, not just in Gower but all over Wales, to seek work in industrial areas that were themselves struggling. A hard time to start a family.

Maria Long married Robert Batcock on the 24th October, 1811, and their first son, Samuel Mansel, was christened on the 4th April, 1813. On the 9th April 1815, a second child was christened – Christopher Long. The second name harks back to Maria's side of the family, in this case her maiden name. At the end of the same month, Maria's brother Samuel's illegitimate son, Thomas Davies Long, was christened and was apparently living in Pwllybrag with the rest of the family. Two years later, on the 17th June, a third child was christened. This was plain and simple 'Robert', so this time his father had his own way with the name. In 1820 (christened 6th June) the Batcocks had their first daughter – Louisa Long, and in 1823 they had another son – Edward (christened 9th February). Little Louisa, just four years old, died and was buried in the winter of 1824 (December 16th) but the Batcocks' next child was a girl and she, too, was named Louisa Long (christened 26th September 1825). It was in 1825 that the matriarch of the family, old Mary Long, died in her 75th year. Another girl (christened 16th October 1828) came soon after this and was named after her mother – Maria. Her mother was, by then, 39 years of age

Interior of Pwllybrag showing the fireplace around which the family would have crowded on cold evenings.

and was, perhaps thinking that the family was big enough. But in 1832 another son was born – Francis Hancorne (christened 25th July). The name 'Hancorne' was a reference to the child's grandmother on the Long side – she was born a Hancorne. At this stage there were at least 10 occupants of the little cottage comprising old David Long, Maria and Robert Batcock and their seven children. Samuel and his illegitimate son may have been there as well, making 12 in all. By any standards, the little cottage was crowded; one can only imagine the constant noise and commotion in a household accommodating the smallest infants, boisterous teenagers and young men, working adults and old David Long. A trying environment for everyone.

Crowded as it may have seemed, the Batcock family grew up in conditions better than those of many in the parish. The Long dynasty, having been established at Pwllybrag for a hundred years, must certainly have acquired at least some basic furniture – a few chairs, a table board, cooking implements and some beds. Outside was a substantial garden and an orchard. There was room for poultry and small numbers of other livestock such as sheep or cattle could graze on the adjacent field or on the common. These could be fattened for market in Swansea or for local fairs. The nearest regular fair was at Penrice on the other side of Cefn Bryn but attempts were made intermittently to revive the old fair at Llanrhidian that was held on the steeply sloping green by the church. In addition, Robert could earn a little money from his professed trade as a carpenter – it seems he could turn his hand to a number of tasks, we shall also see him as part-time glazier and part-time limekiln tender. As a carpenter he might have been expected to be involved in building work such as roof building or he might have made coffins for some of the local people – typical and routine work for a village carpenter.

The Calvanistic Methodist Chapel at Oldwalls (on the left)
with the blacksmith's shop opposite.

The children were fortunate in another way – their school-ing. Education in South Wales was in a parlous state at the turn of the 18th and 19th centuries. Griffith Jones's 'Circulating Schools' were but a memory for most people. Down in Pen-clawdd, with the extra population drawn by industry, there was an even worse situation. The non-conformist church move-ments and, in particular, the Calvinistic Methodists, saw the need and took steps to rectify it. Chapels and Sunday Schools were established at Crofty (Hermon 1807) and Penclawdd (Bethel 1816). The established church did not get involved in this development. The Wesleyan Methodists had been active for many years around Llanrhidian and, about 1813, had estab-lished a little chapel at the hamlet of Oldwalls just west of the village. This chapel had not flourished, however, and quickly became dilapidated. Under the patronage of Lord Barham, William Griffiths, the great Gower evangelist, took over the chapel for the Calvinistic Methodist cause. Possibly a leading light in this was Joseph Allen who lived at Stoneyford on the edge of the moor to the west of Pwllybrag. He was a weaver, born in 1766, who moved to Stoneyford from Welshmoor when his wife died in 1816. He had two daughters – Maria and Elizabeth. It was his elder daughter, Maria, who features in records relating to the school. It seems that the Sunday School was established around 1825 and this shortly became a day school of sorts; in this, Maria was a leading figure. Complimentary remarks by the inspectors, 20 years later, suggest that the school was at the very least 'useful'. It is probable that a combination of evangelistic zeal and downright competence made Maria an effective and efficient teacher. We know from later records that Christopher Batcock could read and write well and, as far as we can judge, the only place he would have acquired those skills was at Maria Allen's academy.

The school was close to the blacksmith's shop in Oldwalls and we can imagine lessons being punctuated by the ring and crash of metal upon metal, the neighing of horses being shod, the shouts of carriers and farmers bringing in broken carts and farm implements. On rainy days, when farm hands might otherwise have been laid off, the farmers would send them to the smithy or accompany them for various maintenance tasks that might be necessary – the blacksmith's then became something of a social centre for the farm workers.

We can imagine the Batcock children wending their way along the moor's edge and through the fields for their daily tuition half a mile away. In summer they would see the cotton grass spreading like white rivers down the slopes of Cefn Bryn, in spring they would hear the larks sing high in the breezy blue sky, in autumn and winter they would walk through curtains of rain sweeping across the moor. On bright days the tide would be blue in the estuary, on cold dull days it would look a drear place. They would pass the men on their way to the fields and the farmers on horseback supervising the work. There was little variation in life for children or adults, each following their apportioned lot towards goals set out for them and in which they had little or no say.

Chapter Two

New Neighbours

In October, 1833, the Batcocks found that they were to have new neighbours. The cottage of Cae Morgan, two fields to the east, was the nearest house to Pwllybrag and it had been acquired by the Reverend John James of Penmaen for his daughter, Caroline, upon her marriage. This marriage took place on the 3rd October, 1833. The bridegroom, Charles Edward Morgan, was a man from a very wealthy family based at Biddlesden in Buckinghamshire. Although the family was English, their more distant roots and much of the source of their wealth were Welsh. Generations before, the Morgan family had inherited lands in the Towy valley around Aber-cothi; they had also received a gift of the tithes of Llanrhidian parish, Higher and Lower. This large parish, stretching nearly half the length and half the width of Gower, was potentially productive of significant income. On the death of his father, Charles Morgan and his five brothers decided to maintain the family estates intact and pool the family wealth. Charles's function in this was to manage the tithe estate in Llanrhidian so he settled, with his new Welsh bride, at Cae Morgan. Clearly, the house was too small and quite inadequate to the needs of a wealthy man and his hoped-for family so an almost complete rebuilding took place. While this was going on, Charles and Caroline lived at Stavel Haegr farm, down by the marsh on the other side of the village.

Charles Morgan did us the inestimable service of keeping a detailed diary for the entire time that he resided in the parish. Meticulously written in a tiny hand to fit the pages of 'Letts' diaries, they record his struggles and successes as well as the business matters that preoccupied him. Each day he wrote some 50 to 100 words about his life as a farmer, gentleman, family man and Gower socialite. He recorded the weather, shopping, market deals and, importantly for us, his neighbours. He leaves little doubt that he felt he had 'drawn the short straw' in having to live in Gower whilst his brothers enjoyed the fruits of more congenial estates in Carmarthen, Buckinghamshire or Kent. At the same time he gives the impression that he brought new ideas and enthusiasm to his farm in Llanrhidian. This was not to the liking of his bailiff, George Eliot; the two seemed to hold each other in mutual contempt. Eliot, probably installed by the committee of brothers Morgan, had had control over the day-to-day running of the estate and the collection of tithes and he no doubt resented the intrusion of this upper class novice. Moreover, Eliot was a wily and clever man who no doubt felt he had the measure of the local people; he probably felt that

Charles Morgan would be exploited by all who had the opportunity to deal with him.

Whilst battling with his bailiff, Morgan also had to satisfy the needs of his young wife, Caroline, learn the art of farming and acquaint himself with the village folk and fellow farmers. He learnt about his nearest neighbour, Robert Batcock, early on. On a wet day in January, 1834, we find Batcock employed glazing the stable windows in Stavel Haegr whilst Morgan is at his accounts and Caroline lies lazily abed. He may have had previous dealings but the diaries do not start until three months of Morgan's residence in the parish had elapsed. Although honourable in his dealings, Charles Morgan was inclined to be reluctant to open his purse and often complained of what we now call 'cash-flow problems'. It is not surprising, therefore, to find that it was May 1st before he paid Batcock the £2 owing for this work and this was on the occasion of Robert having to pay his wealthy neighbour a before-breakfast call. There seems to have been no acrimony, however, and, in discussion, Batcock told Morgan that he was going to live in Swansea. Why Robert should have to consider this is probably a reflection of the times. Work was intermittent, at best, in the parish and he had a large family to support – his youngest child was only two years old. At this stage, Pwllybrag was very crowded with at least 10 people living under its roof and the eldest boys, Samuel, Christopher and Robert were by now young and presumably boisterous adults. Later entries in Morgan's diaries, as we shall see, reveal tensions within the Batcock household and these also may have encouraged Robert to consider living away from home.

Before he made this move, however, there was ample cause for friction with his neighbour. Part of the estate of the Morgan family, at this time, was Penrallt Farm where George Eliot lived.

This farm was just to the west of the village and at the top of the limestone cliff that separates the higher ground of the parish from the marshes of the Burry Estuary. It was on these cliffs that the quarrying activity of the village took place and kilns were built adjacent to the workings to convert the spoil to lime. On Saturday, 15th June, Morgan noted in his diary that *Mr Batcock has a dispute about limestone near new kiln. I desist. He is very bold and defies.* It would seem that there was an argument about who had a right to quarry, and where, but the entry tells us in its laconic style a great deal about Batcock. It is quite possible that Morgan, with his experience previously in the more class-segregated shires of England, had never experienced the lack of deference that Batcock displayed. Conversely, it is not likely that Batcock had found himself pitted against a man of Morgan's background before, so his

Limestone burning kilns were common across Gower and were found on the waste land near Llanrhidian. This reconstruction is based on a surviving kiln at nearby Landimore.

bold and defiant stance suggests that he was far from intimidated. Charles Morgan sought advice from a Mr George who seems to have lived outside the parish and on the Tuesday morning they met at Penrallt. Mr George seemed to think that Robert Batcock had 'no lease' to quarry there – the imprecise language suggests that there was considerable vagueness in this area and that villagers had taken as their right an activity they had carried on for generations. Robert joined the meeting and was not 'over civil'. On the next Thursday, Morgan ordered his men to the 'Kiln Quarry' because Batcock continued to defy on the issue. His account gives the impression that Batcock had probably objected to Morgan's activities there and not vice-versa.

It is interesting that the two men carried on a working relationship, however. On July 17th Morgan attended Penrice Fair over on the other side of Cefn Bryn. It was a quiet affair from his point of view but he managed to sell some pigs and bought a few cattle. On the 1st August he went across to Pwllybrag to pay for these cattle from which we may infer that Batcock had acted as his agent and probably brought the cattle back for him.

Robert Batcock may have had troubles but so too did Charles Morgan. The issue of the collection of tithes was increasingly contentious and there were constant meetings and arguments with the local and regional tithe payers. In addition to this, his first child was on its way and he was the sort of man who shared all his wife's concerns and anxieties in this matter. Early in October, 1834, he took rooms in Swansea anticipating his wife's confinement and wishing to have the best medical advice immediately to hand. Things did not go well and the account of Caroline's labour is harrowing indeed. There was much suffering, both physical and mental, before the child was miscarried so that the mother might live. After some recuperation, Caroline took the boat to Bristol to stay with her sister Jane. In 1835 Charles Morgan discontinued his diary for some 18 months but it can be inferred from the 1837 diary that a second confinement in October 1836 was successful. This confinement took place in the little town of Swaffham in Norfolk where Caroline's father had been curate since 1835.

Back in Llanrhidian, in 1836, the Batcocks had their own sadness to deal with when the grand patriarch of the family, old David Long, died in November. By this time it can be inferred from Charles Morgan's diary that Robert Batcock (senior) had indeed gone off to Swansea to live. Occasionally, at times such as harvest, he appeared to ask for help in the form of carts etc to help carry his wheat. All other dealings with the Batcocks mention only Mrs Batcock who would run errands, ask for advice and deal with farm matters. The chief of these was, to Morgan's mind, the proper upkeep of her hedges. *Bothered to death with Batcock's sheep,* he writes early in 1837, following which we find Mrs Batcock applying to him for the return of the said sheep. Financially she was finding things difficult and soon found herself in debt to Charles Morgan. It seems that she secretly arranged a sale of her farm chattels, presumably hoping that the Morgans would not know of her financial situation or of her inability to pay her debts but Robert Harry, the new bailiff was well up to this and made 'purchases' at the sale to offset what was owed to his master.

It was about this time that we find that the younger Batcocks were beginning to take an interest of another kind in the Morgan household. Charles Morgan, like every well-to-do farmer of the time, had a number of servants working for him, male and female. The female servants were of an age where they might be of interest to young men and their proximity to

Cae Morgan, the residence of Charles Morgan. The present house stands amid many trees planted by Charles Morgan in the 1840's and looks south over the common of Cefn Bryn.

Pwllybrag made them of interest to the Batcocks. The eldest boy, Samuel, is recorded just once, beyond his own birth, in the parish records. In 1834, the birth of a little boy at Pwllybrag is recorded; his name was Alfred and his parents were Mansel Batcock and Anne Bowen. This looks like an illegitimate birth and the father, Mansel, must be Samuel Mansel. Recorded then as a farmer, we find him no more in local records. Of the other Batcocks, the eldest were Christopher and Robert and they seem to have been the main 'predators' in respect of Morgan's servants. Unfortunately, Morgan's diary tends to be unspecific as to which of these was the chief culprit but it may well have been Robert, the younger of the two. One of Morgan's servants, Susan Cornish, came from Swaffham where his baby was born. Charles had visited the town in June and brought back with him his wife Caroline, Charles his son and Susan Cornish whose duties lay mainly in looking after the baby. She, poor girl, just 19 at the time, was quite distraught at leaving family and home to come to the other side of Britain – *she cries terribly at the thought of separation, can I keep her?* is entered in the diary before he left Swaffham. The wrench was made, however, and she settled well into her new job. The other servant, Margaret, was a local girl. She went to Swaffham with Charles and probably helped persuade Susan to come to Wales. Margaret was frequently ill and at times returned to her home in Penmaen to recuperate. Charles Morgan never complained about these illnesses and the family seemed quite solicitous for her. However, Margaret was not happy and, on the 30th October, handed in a month's notice.

On the 20th November, returning from a very late Sunday service (10 p.m.), Charles Morgan was vexed to find the *house*

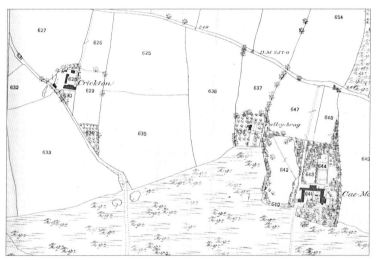

Nineteenth century Ordnance Survey map showing Cae Morgan and Pwllybrag. The highway leading from Llanrhidian to Swansea runs across the top of the map, the common of Cefn Bryn occupies the bottom (south) of the map.
(Reproduced from the 1879 Ordnance Survey map).

open and Robert Batcock at no good in the stall with Margaret. Margaret had left his employ by the end of the month but when, in December, Mrs Batcock requested the use of one of his carts, Morgan felt on this occasion it was appropriate to refuse because her son had *not behaved well*. On previous occasions he had lent cart, horse and man to help with farm work so this was a severe censure.

The censure was not, however, sufficient to deter Robert. No sooner had Margaret departed than he began to show an interest in Susan. On the 4th January, 1838, Morgan found them together late at night. Again, on the first Sunday in February he writes *Caught Batcock again snicking about after the women, gave him a good dubbing*. This was not the main cause for friction with the Batcocks, however. Over the year, Mrs Batcock's farm management was called into question by Morgan time and time again, chiefly on the issue of her animals trespassing on his fields and damaging his crops. When he spoke to her on one occasion he found her full of promises, *very civil, over much*. On the 20th May (1838), he complained of her cows trespassing on his clover and destroying a ducks nest. Earlier in the year, her sheep had been the problem but, the following year, pigs became a major cause of ill-feeling. Maria Batcock's inexperience in farming showed in a number of ways, her failure to maintain hedges was the chief one but, on the 14th December (1838), Morgan notes that she stifled her pigs on her way to Penrice Fair. In spite of the ill feeling that must have existed over these neighbourly problems, the Morgans and the Batcocks got on quite well and would borrow and buy off each other items such as wheat, barm (yeast), eggs, tiles and glass.

The predations of the Batcock men reached a new high in May, 1839. On the 30th of that month, Charles Morgan had taken his family to Ilston. The friends he had proposed to visit in Ilston were, unexpectedly, not at home so Morgan and his family came straight back to Cae Morgan – earlier than the servants thought they would. *Servants surprised at home by our return, lovers there, Batcock lolling on front steps etc.* Morgan wrote indignantly. The next day he made it his business to *chide all the maids severely to tears for their conduct last night admitting Batcock to the House, surprised by our return.* This episode seems to have put an end to the issue for the time being and this was just as well because, from August onwards, Maria Batcock's pigs once more became a source of antagonism. By the beginning of September, Morgan was at his wits' end about the pigs thrashing around in his barley and feasting themselves on his produce. On the 7th he caught *Mrs Batcock's sow* in the standing barley and locked it away with all her litter. *She has done me infinite mischief,* he wrote. Eight days later he discovered *Batcock's pig feasting on my barley, resist shooting at it. Muster my men and confine her.* Two days later he finally prevailed upon her to mend her hedge and grievances were somewhat assuaged.

There is an amusing entry in the diary early in 1840 when, after some severe storms, Mrs Batcock went to church twice, as well as many other 'strangers'. And then, on a Sunday visit to Ilston church, Morgan was surprised to see Mr Batcock attending. That April, Robert Batcock was caught resuming his amatory attentions towards Susan Cornish – *That horrid Batcock surprised by Carree in possession of the house, Susan in the sulks, ergo, lucky I did not see him, I am unhinged in consequence.* Morgan was a man given to irritability and when he stated that he was 'unhinged' he would have been difficult to live with.

By the 29th July, Morgan was threatening legal action against the Batcocks because their horses were damaging his wheat. He impounded them but relented on the same day only to find them in again in the evening. *Angry and speak my mind*

*The Dolphin Inn presided over by the Batcocks. Francis Thomas's
public house, 'The Welcome to Town' can be seen opposite
and higher up the village street.*

to them and threaten an action if fences are not stopped, he writes.
But some change was in the air for, on the 23rd August old Mr
Batcock spoke to Morgan about the possibility of a legacy. Not
long after David Long's death in 1836, Mrs Batcock had sought
advice about his will and this legacy may have related to that.
After David Long's death the Batcocks had taken an interest in
the Higher Mill, a tumble down grist mill next to the church,
and by 1840 they appear also to have some connection with
'The Dolphin', one of the village's two public houses. Whatever
was afoot in this respect, the Batcocks had internal struggles as
well. On the 16th September old Batcock called on Morgan
having been *beaten out of his house by his sons.* Morgan's attitude
towards Robert Batcock seems to have softened. In October,
Batcock's horse died and Morgan saw to it that it was properly
disposed of on the common. Later, in November, when Morgan
killed two rabbits he sent one to Pwllybrag.

The Batcock's, by now, seemed to be more resident in the village than at Pwllybrag. Mrs Batcock appeared to be running the Dolphin public house and, in February 1841, hosted an inaugural dinner of the local 'Felons Association' ('Associations for the Prosecution of Felons' helped support local constabulary in the towns and villages). Charles Morgan was one who attended and complained afterwards that Mrs Batcock's *greens and pudding* had poisoned him – *obliged to go to bed and am really ill,* he writes. Otherwise there seemed to be no friction now between the Batcocks and their erstwhile neighbour until in September of that year real problems did arise. Susan Cornish, the young Norfolk servant, was *discovered in the family way by R. Batcock.* By the standards of the day, this was a moral and social catastrophe. The children, who were very fond of her, were taken from her and she left the house the same night of her own accord to *go God knows where.* This was later found out to be the Dolphin public house. Morgan and his family were all desperately upset about this turn of events whilst his father-in-law, the Reverend John James took it on himself to counsel the offending parties. Robert Batcock promised to marry Susan but the Morgans were anxious that he might renege on this. And Morgan's children pestered him *where is Susan! Poor little things!!!* But Robert did marry Susan, on the 3rd October, and Charles Morgan gave her £2 as a wedding gift. There seems to have been some genuine affection between her and her former employers at Cae Morgan for she was permitted to visit the house and children after these events. Within weeks she went into confinement at the Dolphin but the child was still-born. She must have felt a long way from her distant East Anglian home in those days.

The year being 1841 and a census being taken, it is possible to see in detail how the Batcock family was disposed across the

The Somerset village of Wiveliscombe – unexpected ties with South Wales.

*The bucolic carvings on the Hancock's town house in Wiveliscombe
remind us of the brewery connection.*

The Batcock's, by now, seemed to be more resident in the village than at Pwllybrag. Mrs Batcock appeared to be running the Dolphin public house and, in February 1841, hosted an inaugural dinner of the local 'Felons Association' ('Associations for the Prosecution of Felons' helped support local constabulary in the towns and villages). Charles Morgan was one who attended and complained afterwards that Mrs Batcock's *greens and pudding* had poisoned him – *obliged to go to bed and am really ill,* he writes. Otherwise there seemed to be no friction now between the Batcocks and their erstwhile neighbour until in September of that year real problems did arise. Susan Cornish, the young Norfolk servant, was *discovered in the family way by R. Batcock*. By the standards of the day, this was a moral and social catastrophe. The children, who were very fond of her, were taken from her and she left the house the same night of her own accord to *go God knows where*. This was later found out to be the Dolphin public house. Morgan and his family were all desperately upset about this turn of events whilst his father-in-law, the Reverend John James took it on himself to counsel the offending parties. Robert Batcock promised to marry Susan but the Morgans were anxious that he might renege on this. And Morgan's children pestered him *where is Susan! Poor little things!!!* But Robert did marry Susan, on the 3rd October, and Charles Morgan gave her £2 as a wedding gift. There seems to have been some genuine affection between her and her former employers at Cae Morgan for she was permitted to visit the house and children after these events. Within weeks she went into confinement at the Dolphin but the child was still-born. She must have felt a long way from her distant East Anglian home in those days.

The year being 1841 and a census being taken, it is possible to see in detail how the Batcock family was disposed across the

community. In Pwllybrag lived Robert Batcock senior with
Maria his wife. Also living there were the children Robert,
Edward and Francis together with a labourer, George Harries.
Christopher Batcock was, by now, living in the Dolphin Inn
and described himself as a victualler. With him lived the two
girls, Louisa and Maria as well as a young female servant, Elisa
Williams. The Census took place before the wedding of Robert
and Susan and the diary of Charles Morgan gives the impression that it was to Pwllybrag that Robert took his wife after
their marriage. By what means the Batcocks had been able to
acquire the landlordship of the Dolphin is not at all clear but it
may be that the 'legacy' was an enabling factor.

Chapter Three

Early Misdemeanours

It was not only Robert Batcock who had difficulty repressing his sexual needs. Young Edward Batcock, 21 at the time, managed to seduce Mary Webb of Wernffrwd. Her child, a little girl also called Mary, was registered in Swansea in 1841 under the surname Webb but was christened in Llanrhidian, the following year, as Mary Batcock. At the same time, it appears that Christopher Batcock had also managed to have an illegitimate child. The details of this are completely missing save that Charles Morgan records in his diary (1st June 1843) that *Christopher Batcock's bastard case* was brought before the Swansea Board of Guardians. It would appear that over a period between 1841 to 1842 there were three illegitimate births in the parish that we know of and the Batcocks were responsible for two of them. In addition to these, there was the case of Susan Cornish who was hurriedly brought to the altar in 1841. Christopher's child is almost certain to have been born before 1843 because he was married in 1842. The fact that this matter was being dragged before the town's board of Guardians must, therefore, have been a severe embarrassment to him, especially since his new wife was the daughter of a clergyman.

Maria Phelps, the wife-to-be of Christopher Batcock, was the daughter of the Reverend Robert Phelps of Llanblethian in the Vale of Glamorgan. Llanblethian is a little village just out-side the town of Cowbridge but, although this is the record of the *Cambrian* in announcing the marriage, Phelps was in fact officiating for the church of Llanfrynach, a 'lost village' a little further out from the town. This was a remote and humble calling for a man of the cloth. He had been at Llanfrynach since 1822 but, before that, had been in Somerset in the area round Tiverton and Wiveliscombe. This was where his family was initially brought up.

Llanfrynach Church, a quiet parish in the Vale of Glamorgan.

It is worth considering the small town of Wiveliscombe a little longer since it represents precisely those causes and effects that brought a clerical family of the south west of England into the somewhat different climate of south Wales. Dominating this pretty town today are the buildings of what used to be Hancock's brewery. It was from this sequestered place that the Hancock family invested into a major brewery construction in Cardiff which made them famous and wealthy in the Principality. Links, such as rugby matches, continue to this day between Wiveliscombe and Cardiff. Maria records her birth place as Wiveliscombe (born 1812); her brother was born in Tiverton (1817) and their mother came from Torrington. Robert Phelps married Maria (née Hancorne) at Landough juxta Cowbridge in 1811; it was in this part of the Vale of Glamorgan that her father, himself a man of the cloth, lived.

It is hard to understand how a relatively humble man such as Christopher Batcock managed to woo, if that is the right word, a clergyman's daughter from the Vale of Glamorgan. Christopher was by no means an ignorant man, having good command of reading and writing skills (as we find recorded later). On the other hand, the Reverend Robert Phelps was working in a very humble parish. Maria records herself, nine years later, as a dressmaker; so she was not ashamed to profess a trade. It seems, therefore, that the social divide between her and her husband was not as great as it might have been. But how the two came to meet is a puzzle.

One possible link may have been in the network of the Phelps family; there was a Thomas Phelps born in Llanrhidian in 1771, son of Thomas – was this a possible connection? Another family link that may have existed was in the Hancorne family. Christopher's grandmother (on the maternal side) was

The Somerset village of Wiveliscombe – unexpected ties with South Wales.

The bucolic carvings on the Hancock's town house in Wiveliscombe
remind us of the brewery connection.

Cowbridge Town Hall to where some of the village of Llanrhidian decamped in 1841 and where Christopher Batcock may have met his wife-to-be.

born a Hancorne but she was not originally from the local parish. The name was significant enough, still, to the family for Christopher's youngest brother to have it appended to his first name – Francis Hancorne. Christopher's bride also had Hancorne connections; Maria Phelps's mother, also Maria, was also born a Hancorne although she was born in the distant parish of Torrington in Devon. So the Hancorne family may have been the link between the Phelps and the Batcocks.

Right up to the 19th century, there were close ties with towns, villages and families across the Bristol channel. Water, being relatively easier to travel on than the awful roads of the day, tended to unite rather than to divide people and, in many ways, the people of South Wales were closer to those of Somerset and Devon than they were to their compatriots in North Wales. How Maria's mother came to be born in Torrington is difficult to surmise, however, because her father is later recorded as having been the vicar of Newbridge near Bridgend.

One occurrence which may have led to Batcock meeting his bride-to-be was the large attendance of Llanrhidian parish people at the Cowbridge Sessions which took place in early April 1841. There had been a prolonged dispute between the Higher and Lower Divisions of the parish during 1840. In ancient times Llanrhidian had been one parish but, as the industrial revolution proceeded, the Higher (Penclawdd) division had tended towards a life of its own, quite separate from the rural quietude of its lower counterpart. Gradually, administrative and ecclesiastical arrangements came to reflect that division and it was felt to be clear cut when the case of William Edwards, a pauper, brought the two parts into dispute. The Higher Division believed that the responsibility for maintaining Edwards rested with the Lower Division and vice-versa. The dispute rumbled on over the winter and finally came to settlement at the Cowbridge Sessions. Many people from the village were to be called as witnesses and, at the end of the day, they were successful. It is possible that Christopher Batcock went to Cowbridge on this occasion and there, either by design or accident, may have met Maria Phelps, following which an attachment could have developed between the two.

There was a wedding party, according to Charles Morgan, on the 2nd February 1842 and the wedding itself took place on the 13th, a Sunday. The fact that the wedding took place in Llanrhidian and not in Llanblethian could be an indicator of the Reverend Phelps's disapproval; this may have related to considerations of the couple's relative social standing or even other, untoward, circumstances. The following Sunday Morgan noted, with a hint of wry amusement, that *Mr and Mrs Christopher Batcock* were at church. Presumably, Maria joined Christopher at the Dolphin and may have found the presence of the children irksome. If they had to return to Pwllybrag, this would have put pressure on that household and Robert and Susan would have been the first to feel it. By October it appeared that arrangements had been made to accommodate the family's needs and Morgan noted, with satisfaction on Susan's behalf, that Robert Batcock was to have Pwllybrag. Only four days later, however, he writes with consternation, *Mrs Batcock at last gets Pwllybrag by lying, what's poor Susan to do now?* The solution, it seems, was for the couple to move into the Higher Mill, adjacent to the churchyard. There was probably just enough business for the old, tumbledown mill to keep working and it seems that Charles Morgan did his best to send jobs to the mill whenever he could. As it has been noted before, everyone in the village had some animals to pasture on the marsh and Robert would have done likewise to bolster his income.

The Batcocks were, by now, spread across the parish and village community, residing at Pwllybrag, the Dolphin and the Higher Mill. The circumstances surrounding their marriages, their relationship with the Morgans, their connection with illegitimate births and their abrasive personalities would all have made them well known in the village. An example of the volatility of this widespread and somewhat dysfunctional family is recorded by Charles Morgan early in 1843. On a cold and frosty day in February, Charles had the usual inconvenience of having to impound two of Mrs Batcock's horses for trespassing on his fields. About 9 o'clock, Edward came up to the house *to inquire about his brother Christopher's horses, as he calls them.* Robert and Susan happened to be at Cae Morgan at the time, probably she was looking after the children. Robert made a point of correcting Edward; the horses, he said, belonged to his mother and not to Christopher. *Edward looks and speaks,* wrote Morgan, *as though he would kill one and perhaps will some day.*

There seems to have been some rapprochement between Robert Batcock and Charles Morgan brought about by the regard held by the latter for Batcock's wife. Morgan even seems to have assisted the couple in going to visit her home in East Anglia – her family had by now moved to Bury St Edmunds in Suffolk where they were running a foundry business and apparently prospering. Meanwhile, Pwllybrag seems to have been vacated by the remainder of the family and an Oldwalls man, Thomas Thomas, was installed.

At this time, the Batcock family seemed to be settling down a little, perhaps Charles Morgan thought he was in for a quieter life. But then we find Edward Batcock in trouble again, this time with the law. He had been caught tampering with wood down in the Llethrid Cwm, a narrow wooded valley on the south east corner of the parish. Charles Morgan records, laconically (30th May 1843), *Edward Batcock committed to the treadmill, destroying plantations.* The following month he appeared before Thomas Penrice at Kilvrough House in south Gower on a charge of destroying and damaging underwood. There, a fine was imposed and, the *Cambrian* tells us, it was paid. Possibly, Charles Morgan was mistaken about the treadmill or, perhaps, some peremptory justice had been administered before the case was properly heard.

The Batcock's need for wood was soon, however, to lead them into more open conflict with the community. It had long been a concern of Charles Morgan that the only education available to the village children came from a non-conformist source. The thought that children were not catechised according to the principles of the established church was quite offensive to this very conservative man. In any case, there was nationwide discussion of the need to improve the provision of education as universal enfranchisement and the needs of an industrial society spread. There had been some discussion of the possibility of building schools in both the Lower and Higher Divisions of the parish for some years and, by 1842, sites had been earmarked for schools in Penclawdd and in Llanrhidian. At the same time, using the power of his patronage acquired through the ownership of the parish tithes, Charles Morgan was able to install his brother-in-law, Edward Knight James, into the living of the parish. The Reverend James took a house at Stavel Haegr, the very property where Charles Morgan lived whilst his house was being built at Cae Morgan. Edward James shared Charles's desire to establish the school and, it would appear, greatly assisted in raising the funds for this project. The site chosen was pretty well in the centre of the village, on the hill above the churchyard. By October 1842 the foundation stone was laid but progress, by today's standards, was fairly slow. Although the money for the school was largely raised by subscription, Edward James 'put his hand in his own pocket' on occasions, no doubt to expedite progress. For example, in June 1843, he purchased 23 feet of timber for the carpenter, William David, to work with on the school site.

On Sunday, 11th June, it would seem that Edward James or his carpenter, perhaps both together after the morning service, were looking over the building site when it was noticed that the newly purchased wood was missing. The next day, Edward

James then went up to see his brother-in-law at Cae Morgan to discuss what should be done. They resolved to get a warrant to search for the timber and Edward James went off to secure this. In the evening, Charles Morgan accompanied George Gordon, one of the village constables, on a search of the village. They do not seem to have been long about the search which suggests they were either very lucky or they had some 'previous information' to go on. The wood was found at the Higher Mill in the possession of Robert Batcock. He denied that he had stolen it; later details of the examination of the case suggest he claimed to have 'found' it. In any case, the timber could not be clearly identified as the stolen property since it had been cut up into five separate pieces for use in a door frame. Perhaps the sound of sawing had raised villagers' suspicions when they heard that timber had gone missing from the school. One can only imagine the desperate embarrassment of Charles's servant, Susan Batcock, at the position in which her husband had placed her *vis a vis* her old and respected employer.

The following Wednesday various parties from the village made their way to Ilston village, three miles away, to present their case. Edward Knight James and Charles Morgan rode over at 9.00 am. Two hours later there arrived Robert and Susan Batcock together with the two village constables, George Gordon and William Jone. In addition, the main witness in the case, the carpenter Willam David, also arrived. Morgan does not record the outcome of this meeting but there was clear evidence to press the case so it was presented, on the 27th June, at the Neath Sessions. Mr Tripp, defending Robert Batcock, made an issue of the fact that, whilst the timber was bought by the Reverend James, it more properly belonged to the subscribers. On this technicality, Mr Tripp contended that the

*The village centre from the south west. On the right (foreground) is
the school built by Edward Knight Jamess. Behind it, to the left,
is the old, thatched house of Tir y Merchant and, below that,
The 'Welcome to Town' inn. Based on an old photograph.*

*This old photograph taken from much the same position as the previous
picture but looking north over the church and the marsh. The Higher
Mill was in the bottom left hand corner of this picture.*

property was not properly described and the case not valid. Not surprisingly, this objection was overruled. Robert stuck doggedly to his claim that he had not stolen but found the timber but there was criticism of him for having sawn the timber for his own use – presumably implying that he should have sought the rightful owner first. In the end, however, the impossibility of proving beyond doubt that the timber in Robert's possession was the same as the missing timber from the school made it impossible to secure a conviction and he was acquitted. There seemed to be little doubt in the mind of the court, however, about what had actually happened and, before stepping down from the dock, Robert was warned by the chairman of the court that he had *had a very narrow escape* and the hope was expressed that he *would take it as a warning for the future*.

Sometime between this event and December 1844, Robert Batcock ceased to live at the mill and Christopher, his brother took over there. By this time, Susan's sister Catherine from Suffolk had come to replace her as nurse maid to the children of Morgan's family. She appears to have been very satisfactory to the Morgans in this role and they got on well together. Susan is not mentioned again as playing any part in the household affairs. Indeed, the Batcocks were, by now, a considerable problem to Charles Morgan, if not to the rest of the village. In the space of just two weeks Morgan had seen Edward Batcock committed to the treadwheel, considered Christopher Batcock's case regarding his bastard child before the Board of Guardians and dealt with Robert's alleged theft of his brother-in-law's timber. Thankfully for him, the rest of the year passed without incident as far as the Batcocks were concerned.

Llanrhidian was, by and large, a quiet village, as were most villages in the Gower peninsula. Times were difficult in the

1840's and people must have had their minds set on survival rather than on strife within the community. The disastrous years following the end of the Napoleonic Wars, when there were years without summer, years with drought and autumn storms, had passed. In 1837 and 1838, however, there were more years with dreadful harvests. Things then deteriorated further and, by 1841 there was real hardship in the countryside. The excellent harvest of 1842 was offset by the increasing industrial depression that had begun the year before. Not only did this depress the price of corn crops, it also made it very difficult to sell other farm produce such as butter. If local men sought employment off the land they were to be disappointed – Penclawdd, for example, had little active industry at the time and the mines were not producing coal. In the words of David Williams, historian of the Rebecca Riots, all this 'engendered spiritual malaise and recklessness'.

The tithes became a major source of friction within the parish and must have been greatly resented at this time of depression. Charles Morgan was heavily involved in the negotiations for the tithe settlement; the tithe map for the parish was largely drawn up in his house. The inconvenience to both parties of paying the tithe in kind, a tenth of all produce of the land, irked both sides of the issue. Morgan had very commodious barns to store this produce but would surely have preferred to receive a money payment than haggle over the value of receipts in kind and then sell them on. There was bound to be friction between farmer and tithe receiver in settling these issues but this would probably be exacerbated by the fact that he was not a man of the cloth and that, therefore, these 'taxes' did not directly further the work of the church. Morgan tried his best to accommodate farmers in their difficulties but, at the same time, his brothers were questioning him sharply as to the amount the tithe was eliciting. These were among the conditions that gave Rebecca such fertile grounds to flourish in South Wales. By winter, 1842, the riots had broken out and Gower was as involved as any part of Wales.

There was one major incident locally and that was the assault on the turnpike gate at Three Crosses. This controlled traffic on the turnpike running from Swansea to Penclawdd, the main road running then across the high commons of Gower and not, as it does today, along the marsh edge to Penclawdd. There is a local memory (which fits very well with the facts) that this local riot was fomented in the George Inn in Penclawdd – a building long lost and the site currently occupied by a dental practice on the sea front of the village. The attack was reported to have taken place on the night of Friday, 14th July or rather in the small hours of Saturday morning. At least 60 rioters were reported to have destroyed the gate and a chain protecting it and then to have pulled down an adjoining wall. The toll collector was threatened with death if he so much as peeped out of his window and Mr Eaton, the farmer residing nearby retreated under a volley of stones. The rioters were enjoying themselves greatly and had intended moving on to another gate but the daylight hours were approaching and they had need of the cover of night. The only other gate in the area they could have considered attacking was that at Cartersford Bridge, a little over a mile away on the Port Eynon road but this remained unfinished business. The Cartersford gate took a toll on all traffic proceeding to Llanrhidian and the west of Gower.

The participants in this riot were numerous and very likely comprised small farmers from all over north Gower. Any hotheads with a mind to some gratuitous violence would very likely have come along for some fun, so it is quite likely that folk like the Batcocks were there. Often painted as a reckless and lawless group, Rebecca was not ineffective. It is interesting to note that the Trustees of the Turnpike, at a meeting attended by, amongst others, Charles Morgan, now considered closing some of the gates including the Three Crosses gate. This was in the month following the attack. Morgan makes only passing references to the riots in his diary although one notes that he improved the locks and bolts about his home at the time.

A more interesting, though quite fictional, source for these local events is Amy Dillwyn's novel 'The Rebecca Rioter', published in 1880. Miss Dillwyn, daughter of the eminent Lewis Llewellyn Dillwyn, was born in 1845, two years after these events. However, something of the vivid detail and the sense of alarming times seems to have been transmitted to her by her father who was considerably involved in the struggle against the rioters and was an eye-witness to some of the events. The central character of her tale, Evan Williams, is a young man living in Upper Killay, a rough community on the turn-pike road about three miles out of Swansea on the way to Llanrhidian. He is living in a society which seems to reflect some of the 'spiritual malaise and recklessness' of the times, in her words the people had 'a twist towards wildness'. Farmers passing through this fictional Killay were significantly at risk of being attacked or robbed and one such incident is central to her novel. Men like Charles Morgan had to go to Swansea to bank their money – it was not unknown for him to carry in excess of £400 in his pockets when he rode in to the bank after collecting tithes. Amy Dillwyn draws a picture of two societies – one largely law-abiding and the other whose actions seemed to bear little relation to moral norms. And men like Morgan rode through this 'other' society in places like Killay, not without some qualms. Men like Christopher Batcock seemed to belong to that other society of Amy Dillwyn's and, whether or not they were driven by any moral imperatives, there is little doubt that they felt themselves opposed to their so-called superiors.

The violence of the times is also reflected in Llanrhidian itself. In April 1843, Robert Harry (Charles Morgan's capable lieutenant in the village) found himself in some trouble for an assault on the son of Francis Thomas. Thomas was a local publican of the 'Welcome to Town' and his eldest son was only 16 at the time. More serious, however, was an incident the next year. Charles Morgan paid a visit to old Cornelius Gordon of Cilivor Farm on April 19th in order to see how his son was. This was George Gordon, 45 at the time – it was probably this George Gordon (there were three in the parish) who was the constable in the previous year's case of theft. He had been assaulted by George Edwards and was in bed as a result. There were three George Edwards in the parish, the eldest being the same age as George Gordon; he was the village blacksmith from Oldwalls, opposite Maria Allen's school. A village blacksmith, one imagines, was not a man with whom to fall out. Neither of these cases was actionable but the incident that took place in June 1844 most certainly was.

Philip Morris, a 46-year-old farm hand, probably lived close to the Dolphin Inn in the village where the Batcocks now presided over affairs under the close scrutiny of their mother. It seems that some unpleasant rumour about him was going round the village – reported by the *Cambrian* newspaper as *a scandalous report*. It was his belief that the man who had given the stamp of authenticity to this rumour, if not the main perpetrator in spreading it, was Edward Batcock. In what

A lane in the village.

appears to have been a towering rage, he called at the Dolphin Inn to challenge Edward but he was not there. It may well be that Edward, much younger at age 21, was less than a match for Morris. Morris set off to find the young Batcock; meanwhile Mrs Batcock senior, realising what was afoot, sent for Christopher to support his younger brother.

The *Cambrian*'s report says that Philip Morris shortly found Edward *in a lane near the village.* Judging from the number of people said to have been involved in what then happened, it is likely that this lane was close to the village centre, perhaps just round the corner from the Dolphin although the newspaper account suggests it was a little distance from where Christopher Batcock then resided which was probably at the Higher Mill. On being confronted, Edward denied any responsibility for these scandalous reports and at that stage things became very heated indeed. Both sides claimed to have been the victim of assault but Batcock's account is the more graphic. He said that, after being accosted by Morris, he was struck three times before retaliating. After the second blow he told Morris, 'I will take but one more' – in today's parlance 'You do that again and . . .'. His claimed reluctance to enjoin battle does seem to confirm that that this would have been an unequal struggle at this stage. At some stage, Christopher Batcock arrived in support of his brother. Morris claimed to have been felled to the ground and kicked violently about the body before Christopher arrived. He was then subjected to *great violence* before losing consciousness. When he regained consciousness he found that he had been moved *some yards from the spot where the assault was first committed*. Edward Batcock, on the other hand, claimed that he had been the victim of an assault in which seven or eight villagers had supported Morris as a result of which it was he (Batcock) who had been kicked and beaten while on the ground before his brother came to help.

Whatever the truth of the matter, it was greatly to the detriment of the Batcocks' cause that Philip Morris appeared in court, shortly after the incident, with *several prominent marks of violence about the mouth, eyes, etc.* Witnesses were brought forward in support of Philip Morris. One was George Edward's, the blacksmith's, son William. (There was another William Edwards who lived nearby, just a year older at 16, who might have been the witness but evidence is lacking as to whether he had come to live in the parish by this time.) The other was 71-year-old John Smith from Granada, West Indies and apparently a newcomer to the village. Smith would only confirm that Batcock had begun the violence but both witnesses agreed that the attack had been violent. Sitting in Petty Sessions before Magistrates – Reverend Dr Hewson, Reverend J. Collins, John

Grove and J. H. Smith, a verdict was arrived at after a short deliberation. Both the Batcocks were found guilty and fined 25 shillings (£1.25) and they were ordered to find sureties to keep the peace for twelve months.

In a relatively law-abiding community, villagers were now aware that there was trouble amongst them. This sizeable family, in the space of just a few years, had been responsible for seduction, vandalism, theft and assault. Not only this, they controlled the village inn and one of the local mills, they had eyes and ears everywhere, it seemed. There must have been much fearful conversation behind closed doors and with hand over mouth in those days, possibly even railing at the leniency of the legal system. One imagines the whispers, 'He could have killed him', 'He should have been locked up', 'What's happened to our village?'

Chapter Four

Death at the Turnpike

By 1844, Rebecca was finished. There were no more riots, no more clandestine meetings of men with faces blacked and wearing womens' clothes. But it is impossible to imagine that the memories were anything but fresh and powerful, the grievances still hurting and the objects of hatred still loathed. The year 1844 had been a disastrous one for agriculture, drought and unseasonable storms ruining much of the harvest. Times continued hard. The turnpike gates were marked out by Rebecca as the most particular emblem of the ills that beset the people. To the small farmers and ordinary people who made up the great bulk of the population of rural areas, the turnpike gates were an affront to their human rights. To be denied free passage on the roads was, indeed, a severe imposition on a hard pressed population. Being a peninsula, there was no practical way for Gower folk of avoiding the charges if you wished to take livestock to market or travel by any means other than foot. Those living in Llanrhidian who wished to travel to Swansea would have been obliged to climb out of the village on the road that led past Cae Forgan, across the lower moors of Cefn Bryn and then through fields and moors to the turnpike gate at Cartersford Bridge. This was in a valley between two of Gower's big commons, Pengwern and Fairwood, beside a small but vitally necessary bridge across the Llethrid stream. Thence, climbing a steep hill across Fairwood Common, the road continued through the fields of Killay and Sketty to Swansea. True, the Llanrhidian people could have used the little lane that crossed Welsh Moor to the north, but this was tortuous and muddy near Three Crosses and had a most precipitous hill at Dunvant, both to descend and to climb up from on the other side of the valley, before winding through more woods and fields to join the turnpike road at Olchfa. It was impractical for commercial use.

There was also the suspicion that the gentry fixed the positions of the turnpike gates to their own advantage. For example, the gentry of the mansion of Gellihir (which, as it happened, burned down in 1788) would have found that they could avoid the Cartersford gate by dint of being on the Swansea side of it; locals may well have harboured the suspicion that this was more than an accidental convenience.

Pedestrians, of course, would have been able to pass through the turnpike with no other inconvenience than having to use the side gate provided for them. All other users would need the gate opened on payment of tolls that varied from a penny (about half a modern penny) for unladen draught animals to

The turnpike at Sketty. Ordinary pedestrians would be expected to use the side gate to the left of the picture. Tolls were exacted from all other travellers according to a set of charges displayed on the booth to the right of the picture.
(Picture courtesy of West Glamorgan Archive Service).

three pence (one and a half modern pence) for passenger bearing carts and carriages. Flocks or herds of animals paid up to ten pence (about three and a half modern pence) for each score of animals. Of course, this made the poor toll collectors the most reviled of all those involved in the Turnpike Trusts. A menial job and poorly paid, toll collectors were humble men and by the time of these events it was becoming hard to get men to do the job.

So it was that, in the winter of 1844, on the night of December 21st, two men might have been heard making their way along the road leading from Killay towards Llanrhidian. It was a cold night and clear, the weather being very frosty at the time. The moon was full and casting shadows over the road. Being the Saturday before Christmas, there had been a Christmas Market in Swansea, described by Charles Morgan as *excellent*. Doubtless, our two travellers had enjoyed the market and may perhaps have stopped for a drink or two at the 'Full Moon' at Olchfa or the 'Black Boy' at Killay on their way home. It was getting late and, on this still night, what sound there was would have travelled clearly. An owl from trees above, the trickle of water in the Llethrid brook as icicles formed under the dark bridge, the odd bark from a farm dog in Cartersford Farm just above the gate. And maybe a strain of song from our travellers who were Christopher Batcock and his companion George Edwards. Or perhaps one would have heard some heated renouncing of the turnpike gates, an angry recalling of the grievances of Rebecca followed by some conspiratorial whispering. George Edwards was one of two people in the parish of that name; we have already met George

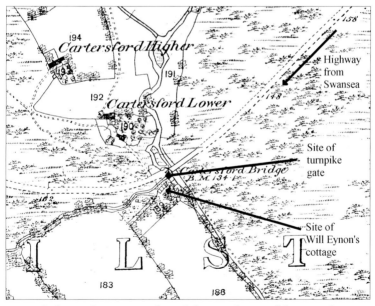

Ordnance Survey map of 1876 showing the site of the turnpike gate at Cartersford.
(Reproduced from the 1879 Ordnance Survey map).

Edwards the blacksmith but this was probably the other George Edwards who was a farm hand at Leason, a hamlet just a mile west of Llanrhidian. This George was just two years Batcock's junior at age 23, much more likely to be a companion to Christopher.

Below the gate, set among a few old oak trees, was a little cottage. It was here that the gate keeper, old Will Eynon, and his wife lived. The remains are still there today, roofless and broken by the trees. Will was 70 years old and hard of hearing. He and Elizabeth, his wife, must have thought it time to turn in for the night, maybe he was just raking over the embers of the fire when she heard a voice shouting 'Gate! Gate!' She indicated to Will to go out and see what was afoot; 'Why do you cry out gate?' he asked, 'You have no horse, can't you go through the side rails'. Elizabeth came out to see what was going on because Batcock and Edwards were getting louder and more insistent in their demands to have the gate opened. 'Damn your eyes, open the gate' shouted Christopher Batcock – Elizabeth recognised him (though she did not know Edwards). Eventually the two men did go through the side gate but, immediately, a scuffle broke out, there was pushing and some waving of sticks. Edwards later claimed that old Eynon had pushed Batcock down the slope of the bank – the road was made up on both sides to cross the bridge at this point. Eynon had his temper up by now and was not prepared to let the matter drop. Edwards said he returned to his house to come out again. The suggestion from the evidence was that he had gone to fetch a marlin spike he kept about the house but Elizabeth disputed this. It was at this stage that Christopher Batcock was seen to bend down, pick up a stone and fling it at the toll keeper who instantly fell, unconscious, in a pool of blood. Batcock and Edwards made off quickly at this point.

Ruins of Will Eynon's cottage at Cartersford.

Elizabeth Eynon rushed off to Cartersford Farm, a hundred yards away, and fetched Morgan Kneath the farmer. He came over and helped carry the senseless man indoors and put him on his bed. The road where he had lain, she said, was covered in blood. Mr Perry, the surgeon, was sent for. This was a long business because he lived over in Reynoldston on the other side of Cefn Bryn. Perry was a sociable man but businesslike as well; Charles Morgan was often surprised at the promptness with which he presented his bills. His attention to old Will Eynon was, however, most assiduous but he could not bring his patient back to consciousness. The stone had struck on the bridge of the nose and Perry feared for the worst.

Christopher Batcock was arrested for the serious assault upon the toll-gate keeper and appeared before the petty sessions the following Tuesday. Charles Morgan noted in his diary, *Serves him right, when will he reform? Never!* Among the four magistrates presiding were the Reverends Dr Howard and J. Collins – they would have familiarized themselves with Batcock earlier that year after the incident with Philip Morris. Mr Perry's evidence was critical because his patient had still not recovered consciousness and his chances of recovery were poor. When the magistrates indicated that the prisoner would be remanded until Eynon's condition could be ascertained fully, Christopher Batcock anxiously offered people to stand as security for him. This was refused, however, and he went into custody.

On the last day of 1844, Will Eynon died and Batcock found himself faced with a more serious charge. On New Year's Day, Charles Morgan was summoned as a juror to attend the inquest on the gate keeper. The inquest was held at Parkmill on the following day (Thursday) and the evidence was gone through again; no new information was brought forward except that Eynon had met his unfortunate end at the hands of Christopher Batcock. What did not help Batcock, however, was that George Edwards gave his evidence in a *very prevaricating and reluctant manner.* Thus, the one man who might have   been able to show that extenuating circumstances should be taken into consideration managed to cast doubt on his own evidence. The jury returned a verdict of 'Manslaughter against Christopher Batcock' and he was committed to prison under the coroner's warrant.

The case came before the Quarter Sessions on Monday, 3rd March. Charles Morgan made a point of being there and took his eldest son with him, seeing it as an educational experience for the nine-year-old boy. Elizabeth Eynon was questioned about the marlin spike which she admitted was brought in from the road a couple of days after the assault. Whilst accepting that it belonged to her husband she appeared to contend that he had not taken it out of the house on that night.

George Edwards said that both Batcock and Will Eynon had sticks and that Eynon had been aggressive in the use of his. But Morgan Kneath said that there was no sign of sticks to be seen afterwards. When the fatal moment came, Edwards said that he was already going home but, on looking back, he saw Batcock stoop down and, the next thing, Will Eynon fell to the ground.

An interesting twist came at the end of the case; Mr Williams, defending, said that Christopher Batcock would have pleaded guilty in the first place but he felt that extenuating circumstances surrounding the event should be heard before sentence was passed. A high risk policy this because he could have been seen to be wasting the court's time but, as it turned out, it was a shrewd move. Batcock was found guilty but the sentence was deferred. But the case that had preceded Batcock's had some bearing on the sentence which was given two days later. It, too, was a manslaughter case but the details would have disturbed Morgan's little boy if he heard them. John Harries, aged 22, had been one of a dozen miners who attended the house of Edward Rowe in Merthyr on the night of the 8th January (a Wednesday night). Although not a public house, by some means half a cask of beer had been procured and the colliers set about consuming the contents. Between six and seven o'clock, John Harries got into an argument with one Evan Jones. High words were spoken and a scuffle ensued. Both parties lunged and dragged around the room and ended up outside; a few of the colliers went out to watch. Harries seemed to be getting the worse of things, the two were separated and Jones was seen to be looking rather weak. It appeared, from the evidence, that Harries had managed to stab him without being seen by those around. When he was looked at more closely, it was apparent that Jones had been stabbed three times, once in the groin, once in the area of the bowels (which were protruding from a three inch wound) and once in the ribs. When he saw the evidence of what he had done, Harries was heard to say, "Oh God, I've killed him, I've killed him." His friend, David Harries told him to hold his tongue for fear that he would incriminate himself further. Poor Evan Jones, whilst apparently responding to treatment, died ten days later. The weapon that had been used was found and this was produced as evidence – the case was clear-cut and the verdict 'Guilty'.

Harries and Batcock were brought to the bar together on Wednesday morning for sentencing. The judge remarked on the similarities and differences in the two cases. Whilst both had been responsible 'for the death of a fellow creature' in only one case had a deadly instrument been used. In fact, the Judge observed, Batcock had clearly not 'intended to cause any injuries as very serious as death' whilst John Harries had used a deadly weapon ('a crime dreadfully increased of late years') not once but three times and each in a way that might cause death. On the other hand, Batcock had sought and commenced the quarrel that had led to Eynon's death. In spite of the modern perception of the harshness of Victorian sentences, the Judge's decisions were remarkably comparable to those of the present day. Harries was sentenced to transportation of seven years. Christopher Batcock was sentenced to one year in prison with hard labour.

Nine months later, Will Eynon's widow Elizabeth was also dead. Meanwhile, Maria Batcock, Christopher's wife, had to struggle on as best she could. Perhaps, her marriage was not turning out quite the way she had expected. As we have seen, Maria came from a quiet and pretty village in west Somerset – Wiveliscombe. By the time she was five the family was living in Tiverton, the nearest town, where her father was probably acting as curate. When she was ten, the family moved to the

South Wales village of Penllyn in the parish of Llanfrynach near
Cowbridge. This was even more rural than Wiveliscombe in
spite of the proximity of the burgeoning industrialism of the
coalfield. Coming to Gower, perhaps with the blandishment of
having some status in one of its villages, she would have been
justified in not expecting to find her husband in gaol for
manslaughter within three years of moving there. What her
parents thought of this matter is difficult to tell but they could
scarcely be happy for their daughter even if they had regarded
her as headstrong in marrying Batcock. Her source of income
must have been from helping to keep the family business in the
Dolphin. On the 17th January 1845, Charles Morgan notes
that he and his wife visited Maria Batcock and paid her one
shilling and sixpence (7p), also noting that she was going
to Swansea. So she did not run home to Llanfrynach but
continued in the village and, presumably, visited her husband.

Swansea gaol was not the building we see today – a well-
built, forbidding, Victorian statement of attitude towards
crime. Had he gone to prison 20 years earlier, Christopher
Batcock might have expected to be flung into the dungeons of
Swansea Castle. It was only in 1829 that the Bridewell, very
close to the site of the present prison, was built. This was
certainly an improvement in conditions for the prisoners even
if quickly found to be inadequate for requirements. It was a
building shaped as a half octagon with ten wards and exercise
yards and two 'airing yards'. In all, there were 62 cells and two
infirmaries. The first governor, William Cox, leased some land
adjacent to the prison on which food crops were grown to feed
the prisoners. The nickname derived from this garden for the
prison, 'Cox's Farm', still has currency today. Batcock would
have made good use of the treadmill there that his brother had
mounted just a couple of years earlier. Whole days could be

spent on the treadmill which actually had some therapeutic value for the prisoners by keeping them exercised and occupied when they had little else to do.

In the two decades prior to Batcock's conviction, the number of prisoners in Britain had doubled; this was a source of alarm to the authorities. Nor was this an urban phenomenon; trials and convictions in rural areas had risen at the same rate as in towns and cities. In the 1830's the south of England had been convulsed by the Captain Swing riots and the crimes of incendiarism that accompanied them. The Rebecca riots in Wales were probably seen as part of that trend of social unrest but the crimes associated with Rebecca presented problems in respect of management of the penal system. In particular, prisons were seen as part of the problem; it was thought that if they were effective they would be changing criminal behaviour and deterring the populace from further reckless acts. There was special concern about the way in which prisoners were able to communicate with each other and, it was believed, that if prisoners could be restricted in the influence they could have on each other they would become more reflective on the error of their ways. Arrangements inside gaols concentrated on means of isolating prisoners and, where they had to congregate for excercise or for other purposes, controlling or stopping communication between them.

The new degree of control that was required over prisoners led to the building of new prisons that facilitated visual and physical oversight. Pentonville in London, built in 1842, exemplified the new approach with wings radiating from a central control area enabling visual control. Sufficient cells were built to manage solitary confinement for prisoners and all periods out of the cells were tightly controlled. Swansea prison was not built to sustain such a level of control but the ethos of the day probably extended to the governor and gaolers being overbearing by design.

Christopher served his sentence and, by March 1846, was to be seen once again about the village. The mill business had slipped, however, in his absence. Robert, who might have been expected to help out in the mill, had actually gone to Bury St Edmunds (probably with Susan) for some of the time his brother was in prison. Debts had mounted, although Charles Morgan, not a man to harbour grudges, lent the couple some money to pay rent arrears. This record appears in his diary just five days after he noted, on 25th March, that the Batcocks had been turned out of the mill and another installed in their place. So Christopher Batcock, having learned a lesson or two in prison, returned to his community to find matters a great deal more difficult than when he had left. It may not have been in his nature to settle down and make ends meet but that is what he appears to have done.

Chapter Five

Life in the Village

In his absence from the village, how much did Batcock miss the familiar landscape of his home? In an area now recognized as one of 'outstanding natural beauty', Llanrhidian has a special, quiet, beauty all its own. In winter, wet and bleak, the marsh and the moors blasted by ferocious winds and driving rain; it may be difficult to convince an outsider of its charms. But as spring makes its way a difference comes over the whole area. The marsh, dun and muddy for months, takes on a spectacular greenness in the fitful sunlight. The sheep look grateful for the easing of the grazing conditions, the wild birds on the sands can be heard a mile or so away, warbling in their thousands and, every so often, rising in great clouds of flashing white and black. Waders fly purposefully, low across the rippling waters as the breeding season begins. Across the fields there is the glory of the blackthorn bloom followed by the may, billowing white and white-pink down every hedgerow. Even on the moors below Cefn Bryn, a carpet of early flowers – the yellow ladies slipper and the gorse and the purple ling, spread across the ground. In summer the eye is taken by the rivers of cotton grass that follow the lines of wet down the flanks of the hill. The drier ground makes excellent pasture for sheep and cattle that stop the furze and bog myrtle from overwhelming the common. In the balmy summer the flies buzz and bite, the sheep come off the moor and marsh for shearing. In the 19th century the farmers' carts were now trundling laden to market as the produce of the fields increased. Then there was all the expectation and anxiety of the harvest, the constant worry that the weather would turn before the corn was dry, the overwhelming thankfulness if the elements favoured a bountiful reaping. And, as autumn stole in, presaging the bleakness of winter, the snipe returned to the moors, the winter duck to the marshes. The huntsman got down his gun and the cottager gathered logs from the dank woods edging the marsh. The modern eye views all this through a slightly sentimental lense and so too, perhaps, did Christopher Batcock if he had a feel for such things as he languished in prison.

In returning to the village and trying to re-establish some semblance of normal life, Christopher Batcock faced an uphill task and some difficult moments. His younger brother, Robert, had meanwhile spent some time in Bury St Edmunds with Susan and his in-laws. When Christopher came out of prison, Robert returned home, alone. Maybe there seemed more sense in trying to establish some future opportunities for himself and Susan, maybe there were tensions between the two. By trade, he was documented as a moulder at the time and this may imply that he was working in industry in Penclawdd or further away in Swansea. His in-laws were foundry workers and it was probably at Bury St Edmnds that he learnt his skills as a moulder. However, on the 17th April he died at home in the village. Francis, his younger brother, who was present at his death gave the cause as 'inflammation' but this does not appear to be a condition attested by a doctor. Susan was still in Suffolk and probably did not manage to attend the funeral which was held on the 21st April. Charles Morgan was authorized to fetch Robert's box from Swansea which suggests that that was where he was employed. Having softened in his attitude to Robert and Susan, Morgan entered in his diary *poor Robert Batcock dead*. Susan did return for a few months and was to be seen, on occasions, in attendance on the Morgan family who continued to show some kindness to her. But shortly she faded out of local life and returned to Suffolk where she lived for the rest of her life . She never married again.

Christopher also had in-laws to consider in the village. By an extraordinary coincidence, the *Cambrian* newspaper reported, on the same day as Robert's death, the death of Christopher's brother-in-law, Thomas Phelps, in the faraway port of Monte-video. So Maria Batcock, whilst attending Robert's funeral at Llanrhidian would doubtless be thinking of her own brother's lonely demise thousands of miles away.

From the date of Christopher's marriage we also find John Phelps, his brother-in-law, living in the parish. Very shortly after this, Charles Morgan began to receive anonymous letters accusing his bailiff, Robert Harry, of having an adulterous affair with a married lady of the village. Morgan racked his brains as to who would be sending these letters. Likely candidates came to his mind, but none of them had sufficient command of

English to write so well. John Phelps was one he suspected, probably for acting as amanuensis rather than as author of the letters. After a few weeks the matter seemed to 'blow over' and nothing more is heard of the Phelps until 1845. Phelps was an exciseman which must have involved working chiefly in Penclawdd where the little port still operated – exporting coal and importing minerals for the metal works. In April 1845, Morgan received a begging letter from Mrs Phelps 'in great distress'. We may assume that she was either frequenting the village or living in it by this time; this seems strange since her husband still had the cure of souls at Llanfrynach and Penlline near Cowbridge. The most likely explanation is that the Reverend Robert Phelps, 67 years old and with only 4 years to live, may have been in poor health and this occasioned her to need more funds. Morgan lent her 10 shillings (50p).

The following year, John Phelps married Jane Jones and settled in the village. She lived next door to the Higher Mill in a little cottage next to the churchyard. Her father, George Jones, owned a few cottages in the village as well as being a small time farmer. Their first child was born just six months after the wedding (born September 1846). The child was named Thomas George Phelps. As a member of Maria Batcock's family, this would have been a welcome addition to her life in the village although her mother may have been frosty about the earliness of the young Thomas Phelps's birth.

In 1847, George Jones, the farmer's son from Leason who had been installed in the Higher Mill in place of the Batcocks, appears to have returned to farming. It is probable that he could see there was little future in the old building. The Lower Mill, run by William David, was a much newer building and did not have the overhead costs of maintaining a ramshackle old building like the Higher Mill. So it was that we find

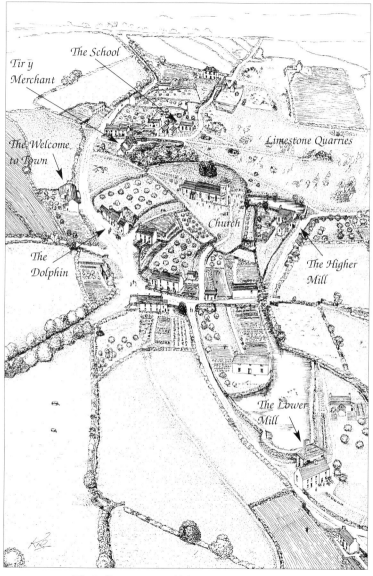

Tir y
Merchant

The School

The Welcome
to Town

Limestone Quarries

Church

The Dolphin

The Higher
Mill

The Lower
Mill

The Village as it would have looked about 1850.

Christopher Batcock and his wife installed in the Higher Mill by the middle of 1847. At about this time, William David in the Lower Mill passed away. Although his wife took over, there may have been an opportunity for Christopher to acquire a little extra business if William David's widow found it difficult to cope. Also in that year, Christopher's youngest sister became a mother. We presume that she had left home sometime before this. The record finds her in Keswick, far away in Cumberland. There, she was giving birth to a baby boy – Mansell Tregurtha. The father was a Cornishman and an engineer. Doubtless it was something to do with mining that took the pair up to the north of England. In 1849 the couple married and we next find them (1851 Census) living in Stoke Damerel near Exeter. They had another two children – James and Louisa.

A further example of Christopher's rehabilitation into local society was his acceptance into parish vestry discussions; he

The Lower Mill of Llanrhidian, one of Gower's most charming examples of vernacular architecture.

became, in effect, a member of the local parish council. He found himself rubbing shoulders with the great and good (as well as some of the more lowly) members of the community. His colleagues on the council were the likes of John Dunn, a well established farmer in Leason hamlet (a mile to the west of the village). There was also John Jenkins, a farmer from Park-y-rhedyn near Charles Morgan with big flocks of sheep on the marsh. Another councillor was William Davies of Llanelen Farm a mile to the east and one of the best established farms in the area. Obviously the Reverend Edward Knight James and his brother-in-law, Charles Morgan, also attended as well as more humble tradesmen such as William Thomas, the local tailor. How was it that an ex-inmate of Swansea Gaol found himself accepted in such company? The answer is simple – the 'vestry' meetings were usually held in the bar of the Dolphin public House, presided over by Christopher's father, Robert. For that reason, it was usual to see both their signatures appended to minutes of Vestry meetings although, by this time, Robert's was beginning to look a little shaky. He was now in his mid-sixties and a relatively old man. He was still capable of practising his trade, however, and in 1849 we find Charles Morgan paying him for putting glass in the chancel window.

Much of the business of the Vestry involved fairly mundane matters such as checking the accounts of the overseers or attending to the maintenance of the church, the highways and parish properties such as the local poor house. Although most meetings were held in the Dolphin, a significant number were also held in the Welcome to Town, the hostelry of Francis Thomas, a few yards up the road and opposite the Dolphin. This was understandable since patronage of the Vestry meant some income from beer sales, typically three shillings and sixpence (18p) for a meeting. Occasionally the meetings were contentious, especially so when an unfair drain on the local economy was suspected as in the earlier case (1840) of the pauper William Edwards. But it was probably not regarded as contentious when Christopher proposed to the Vestry (5th December 1849) some alterations to footpaths around the churchyard that would convenience local people.

Adjacent to the south east corner of his mill pond, and therefore adjacent to the churchyard, was a splendid spring of water that still issues today a plentiful and consistent supply of water. To gain access to this spring, villagers had to pass along a path running north of the church, cross into Christopher Batcock's mill ground and traverse the length of his property

Batcock's Stile next to the graveyard.

and thence reach the spring. This was both inconvenient to the villagers and intrusive for Batcock although he did not complain about intrusion at the meeting. The vestry minute records that it was proposed to divert the path *to accommodate Mr Christopher Long Batcock who has commenced to make a road on the south side of the said pond (the Higher Mill pond) – as he alleges for the greater convenience and accommodation of the parishioners in obtaining water at the fountain head.* This was to be at the sole expense of Christopher Batcock and would also entail the removal of the stone stile to match the footpath coming along the south side of the pond. Although it was probably thought proper to write the minute in the precise language chosen, there does seem to be an air of suspicion in the phrase *as he alleges* and one senses that the Vestry meeting was observing that it was not the convenience of the general parishioners that was principally exercising the mind of Christopher Batcock. The stile is till there, a solid testimonial to Christopher Batcock's 'philanthropy'.

Business seemed to be 'ticking over' at the mill. Charles Morgan, for one, put some work in the way of the Higher Mill. The 'down' side of this, for Morgan, was that Batcock would present himself at Cae Morgan to perplex him with figures suggesting what was owed to him. His diary entry on March 6th, 1849, reads *At accounts, with Christopher Batcock all the evening, he puzzles me with his multitude of balances. Settle with him tomorrow morning.* Not only was he dealing with Christopher but also Mrs Batcock whose accounts, doubtless, related to costs incurred at the Dolphin. And then there was 'Nanny Batcock' who was employed on numerous occasions – this may well have been young Maria who was 19 years old at this time.

Young Edward Batcock had, by this time, made his way to the sea to follow some sort of nautical profession. When he made this departure is not known to us but we do know that, in summer 1850, his father was acquainted with the sad news of his son's demise at sea. His, by now, very shaky signature was appended to papers of administration which were granted in September 1850.

In the same year, Charles Morgan was making preparations for his more-or-less permanent departure to Sherborne in Dorset. Whilst maintaining Cae Morgan as a working farm. Morgan wished to decamp to Sherborne to further the education of his children. It was also a means of entering something like retirement – he was 54 at the time. He continued to make some lengthy visits to Llanrhidian but never interacted with the village in the way he had up to 1850. His last dealings with Christopher Batcock date from August, 1853. He noted then – *Batcock calls about some old accounts for stones and is impudent, turn him out of the house, he says he will never enter again. I hope he may not – openly or by stealth.* In 1855 there appears to have been some difficulty with Christopher regarding changes he was making to the millpond and the effect on the churchyard. The two men exchanged words politely on this last occasion and Batcock agreed to make good any damage done.

In January of 1849, old Robert Phelps died at Llanblethian, aged 71 years. Presumably, his widow Maria took up permanent residence in the village from this time and was found, in the 1851 census, living close to the Dolphin Inn with her son Robert who was now 34. Of John Phelps there was no sign. In March of 1853 Maria Phelps passed away and life became a good deal lonelier for her daughter Maria. A cause for some celebration, later in the same year, was the marriage of the youngest of the Batcock clan, Francis, to a local girl – Elizabeth

The millpond of the Higher Mill next to the churchyard.
Batcock's stile can be seen just to the right of the two trees.

Thomas. The wedding took place in Swansea parish church. Married in September, sadly she lived only until June of the following year. Clearly, she was consumptive when she married and died of 'phthisis'. Another sad loss to the Batcock family was that of Christopher's sister, Maria, who also died of consumption in May 1855, she was just 27 years of age. She had been declining for some years and was said to have borne her illness 'with fortitude'. It may be that she had been disappointed in a love affair, to add to her woes, since her mother ran into debt about this time over the 'intended marriage' of one of her daughters. Or, perhaps, the expectation of marriage was cut short by Maria's untimely death. Life was fragile in the country as well as the town.

'The Felon's Association for the Prosecution of Criminals' continued through the 1840's after its inauguration in February 1841. This was partly an annual social gathering and partly a means of raising funds for the institution of a village police constable. The first meetings of the Association were held in the Dolphin Inn – it was one such occasion that led to Charles Morgan complaining of Mrs Batcock's cooking. As the true nature of the Batcock family became more apparent to the villagers, it seemed that the incongruity of holding the Association meetings in the Dolphin became more obvious. In 1844 we find that the Association had moved to the 'Welcome to Town' under the more sedate stewardship of Francis Thomas. This did not meet with the approval of all and one friend of Charles Morgan, Mr Holland (probably the farmer of Manselfold), decided to have his dinner on his own in the Dolphin, *with a real felon* as Morgan put it in his diary.

Christopher might have been justified in feeling no longer a felon by the 1850's. He had been accepted into the fabric of local life, had assisted in the local administration and ran a passable mill business. His griefs and losses, as well as causes for celebration, showed him to be a man like any other in the village. By his 40th birthday he appeared to be a law abiding and hard working man in a typical rural community, putting the past behind him.

Chapter Six

'A Charge of some Novelty and Seriousness'

In Penclawdd it was said that the pervasive sound of the village was that of donkeys braying. Donkeys were the mainstay of the cockle industry in the area and their cacophonous braying on the hillsides above the village would keep people awake right through the night. Further down the estuary, in Llanrhidian, a gentler animal sound pervaded. Sheep in their hundreds, across the marshes, in the fields and through the lanes. Most men in the village farmed in a large or a small way. One of the village lanes was called 'Ship Lane', derived from 'Sheep Lane'. The easiest way to farm was probably with sheep because of the immediate proximity of the marsh. Christopher Batcock had fifteen sheep that he kept on the marsh and, from time to time, he could be seen driving his little flock up or down the lane leading between the Higher Mill and the marsh.

George Harris was the first to notice. He was from Walterstone, a farm up on Cefn Bryn, and was shepherd to the farmer there, Robert Davies. It was about one o'clock on a Saturday afternoon (August 4th, 1855) that had looked set to continue the recent rainy spell but had then cleared up very nicely. George stepped into a gateway near the bottom of the village, probably just below the Dolphin, to allow Christopher and Francis Batcock to bring their sheep up from the marsh to the Higher Mill. It was lamb shearing time for Christopher, and he needed his flock at the mill that day, he said. They may have passed pleasantries about the improving day. George Harris, earlier in the year, had helped Christopher shear his little flock so he would have been surprised to see him bring upwards of 20 sheep in. Suddenly, a lamb jumped out from the middle of the flock; Francis went to retrieve it. George pointedly told the Batcocks that the lamb might as well be let go back to the marsh – it wasn't theirs. 'No, its mother's in the flock,' Francis told him. Harris had been shepherding on the marsh for eleven years now and knew what he was talking about – 'No, she's not in the flock,' he told Francis. 'Whose is it then?' he asked. 'John Jenkins's,' Harris replied. Jenkins of Park-y-rhedyn Farm had large flocks (upwards of 200) on the marsh and Harris noticed several of his sheep in the flock. Perhaps not wishing to argue with a man who had just recently lost his wife, Harris turned away and went off to have his dinner.

On the other side of the lane from the Higher Mill, and a few yards below it, was the probable home of the village shoemaker – Thomas Thomas. One can imagine that, about lunch time after a hard morning at the last, he would lean against the garden gate and draw on his pipe, watching the

*The lane leading past the shoemaker's cottage (right)
to the Higher Mill (centre).*

world go by. If he saw Christopher passing by with his sheep, he would doubtless have passed the time of day, commiserated with him on the recent loss of his sister and his sister in law, philosophized on fate and talked about how the weather was 'turning out nicely'. As Thomas Thomas looked over his garden gate that day, he probably said as much to Christopher and Francis Batcock as they drove their flock of sheep up to the mill. A further pull at his pipe, a swat at the midges biting on his neck and he looked at the flock as it passed by. After some ten minutes Francis reappeared, driving three sheep that did not bear the mark of Christopher Batcock. He passed by, apparently taking them back to the marsh. Thomas now became suspicious; on the face of it, Batcock had accidentally rounded up some sheep that were not his and returned them to the marsh. Very probably, one of them was the same that George Harris had commented on. Thomas had not made a point of counting the number in the flock that had passed up ten minutes earlier but, perhaps on recollection, it was more than eighteen (which would have comprised all Batcock's sheep together with the three later returned to the marsh). Perhaps something else was also playing on his mind, a nagging and long-standing suspicion.

Later, Thomas Thomas and George Harris got together and compared notes. At least one of the sheep belonged to William Thomas, a village mason, and he too was brought into the discussion. He lived in Tyr-y-Merchant, right in the heart of the village, on the green, and a neighbour to the Dolphin. Also included was Thomas Gwyn, a weaver. After some discussion, William Thomas and others decided to keep a watch on the Higher Mill that night.

Christopher and Francis were drinking late at the Dolphin that night for, when the rest of the village was abed, they had work to do. Unknown to them, a vigilante group had gathered at the mill. At half past eleven, seeing no sign of life in the village, the Batcocks adjourned to the mill. It was a clear, moon-lit night and the watchers could well see what was happening around the mill. About midnight, a light was to be seen in the basement of the mill. At some little risk to life and limb, some of the watchers had climbed into the mill wheel itself. From the bottom of the wheel they could peer into the cellar and there they saw that sheep were being slaughtered. Christopher was holding a candle and Francis was going about the butchering of a number of carcasses, some of which were hanging to one side. The watchers took it in turn to look in at the grisly scene. From time to time, one of the Batcocks would leave with a bucket and was seen throwing things in the stream. Observers secreted in the shoemaker's cottage opposite saw something larger being placed in the drying kiln adjacent to the mill building. Finally, about half past one in the morning, the Batcocks had gone and the watchers hauled themselves out of their uncomfortable observation point. In itself, what they had seen was no crime, but the next morning a search was made of the marsh and all of Batcock's fifteen sheep were to be found calmly grazing the marsh's green sward in the sunshine. William Thomas must have been fuming, he had but recently purchased his sheep at Neath Fair and valued them at ten shillings (50p) each. He immediately suspected that one of these sheep had been taken by Batcock. The village constable, PS Thomas Jones, was applied to and, on the arrival of his assistant, the Higher Mill received an official visit. It appears that William Thomas was present at this stage because he later testified that Christopher Batcock had called him back to the house and admitted that 'the meat was in his workshop'. This may have been an attempt to get Thomas to call off the search but matters had gone too far by now. Meanwhile the constable began his search. Jones

The ruins of the higher Mill during rebuilding on the site. The pipe in the background fed water to the mill wheel in which the villagers hid. In the foreground is the basement in which the butchering took place.

received some praise for the assiduousness with which he carried out his investigation and this praise seems well deserved. In various parts about the building, the constable found three sheeps' heads, three sheeps' skins and 'other portions of the sheep'. The distinguishing blacking or pitch marks by which the ownership of the sheep could be established had been carefully removed so the discovery of the ears, which also marked the owner through the clipping process, was vital. Unfortunately, the ears had been chopped into little pieces. These PS Jones found in the stream which, by a peculiarity of this mill, ran under the mill building. Asked where the meat of the animals was, Batcock was particularly prevaricating. He first asserted that it was in the Dolphin, then offered to fetch it or to accompany the constable. Then changing his mind he told the constable to remain while he (Batcock) fetched it. PS Jones had had enough nonsense by now and handcuffed both Christopher and Francis. The meat was then found in the joiners shop on the upper floor of the mill. Jones felt he now had sufficient evidence to arrest both Christopher and Francis Batcock who were detained the same day.

William Thomas and his friends were anxious that, in condemning one of their fellow villagers, they had their facts absolutely right. The marsh was scoured for any trace of the missing sheep but it was not to be found. The shoemaker had seen two other sheep being led away with the Batcocks' sheep the evening before, one belonging to a Mrs Thomas in the village and the other to Samuel Jones, a farmer in Leason hamlet. But PS Jones's evidence suggested the other two sheep that had been killed belonged to John Jenkins of Park-y-rhedyn Farm who had large numbers of sheep on the marsh. He was not in the habit of counting his sheep, even at shearing time, and appears to have gone out on the marsh as little as possible.

Sheep on the marsh near Llanrhidian, Llanmadoc Hill in the background.

PS Jones asked him to ascertain whether he had lost any sheep but he failed to do this, hardly surprising since he had no means of verifying a loss.

The case was brought before a court on the following Tuesday and the initial evidence, according to Charles Morgan who was in the village for the harvest season, was compelling. The two brothers, to Morgan's obvious disappointment, were *remanded only*. The case was then brought before a full court on 10th September with William Thomas and John Jenkins as prosecutors. The *Cambrian* newspaper reported the case as *a charge of some novelty and seriousness*. The court room was packed on the two days of the hearing (Monday and Thursday). The Batcocks were described as 'well-known' in Gower and, of course, a sheep stealing case could well attract a severe penalty although, since 1832, the death penalty had been abolished in respect of sheep stealing.

Mr Tripp, for the prosecution, was hearing the details of the case for the first time at the initial hearing. He seemed a little put out at having this case entrusted to him at short notice. At first, much hinged on the pitch markings of the sheep. Batcock's defence had not been prepared by his counsel but it seems that he protested that he had more than fifteen sheep and that, therefore, the sheep that were slaughtered were his. In addition, he implied that he too experienced losses of sheep, maybe the culprit was still at large. William Thomas also commented that he had lost sheep before and a picture seemed to develop of a history of sheep going missing in recent years. Batcock's mark was in lampblack, 'a streak commencing on the middle of the back going over the loin, and ending by the hind leg on each side'. William Thomas's mark was a circle on the side and a pitch mark 'WT' on the rump. John Jenkins marked his sheep with a pitch mark 'J' on the 'near side'. The ears were marked with a 'fork' (off ear) and a 'spade' and a 'halfpenny' on the near ear. In shearing off the wool that held these marks, the Batcock brothers were alleged to have been less than proficient because the shape of the marks was echoed by the area shorn off. William Thomas swore that the mark cut off one skin was a circle 'because the place where it has been cut off is round'. Jenkins was less adamant about his marks although he thought it most likely that the letter would have been exactly where the wool had been shorn. He was more confident that the ear marks were clear evidence of his ownership. On the whole, Jenkins was a poor and reluctant prosecutor of his own case and this must be because it reflected that he was very casual in farming practices.

George Harris was more useful to the prosecution. He had assisted Christopher Batcock in shearing his sheep earlier in the year and testified that he only had fifteen sheep then and that he could only find fifteen sheep on the marsh after the alleged theft. According to him, Christopher had never complained of any loss of sheep. PS Jones gave clear and unequivocal evidence.

Not only had he amassed sufficient evidence to establish the nature of the crime, he had got his assistant to reassemble 10 pieces of one ear to make a 'perfect ear' from which the clip marks could be seen. Because the hearing took place over two days, there was some question as to whether the Batcocks should be released on bail at the end of the first day. Mr Tripp, for the prosecution, strongly opposed this. Instead, he asked for, and obtained, the binding over of all the witnesses (and their counsels) in the matter of £40 each, to ensure attendance at the Thursday hearing. Clearly he had received indications that some witnesses might become reluctant to attend in the interval – a clear suggestion of the potential for witness intimidation. What appears to have been a furious exchange followed between the bench and the defending counsel, Mr Howard. In applying for bail he intimated that if the bench refused he would apply to a superior court. The bench responded by immediately refusing bail, stating that it was ready to give its reasons if requested. On Thursday the case was completed and both the prisoners were committed to the next Quarter Sessions for sheep stealing. As they 'went down', one can imagine Christopher saying a big 'thankyou' to his counsel.

Sheep stealing was not such an uncommon crime in those days, nor was it particularly commonplace. Reading the pages of the *Cambrian* newspaper, the great organ of communication around Swansea and West Wales in those days, there were plenty of cases of sheep theft. In 1810 and 1811 there were three cases (in Montgomery, Haverfordwest and Caernarvon) that resulted in the death penalty for the offender. One of two cases heard in Cardiff in 1813 also resulted in the death penalty. The case of Griffith Williams in 1817 resulted in the death penalty but this was later remitted to a year's imprisonment. This also happened in the higher division of Llanrhidian parish, the following year, when Edward Coleman of Rhean Fawr Farm (near Three Crosses) was reprieved from hanging for the theft of about 100 sheep. That year, 1818, had a serious outbreak of sheep stealing and the authorities once more took to draconian penalties; two of the cases resulted in the death penalty being administered. After that, the use of the death penalty was quite exceptional. Sheep stealing became much less frequent and, in the years around the Rebecca riots, almost unknown. A typical case that occurred locally was that of Morgan Thomas of the neighbouring parish of Llangennith in 1838-9. In this case, Mr Joseph Gwyn of the large farm of Townsend in Landimore was in the practice of pasturing his sheep on the common land of Llanmadoc Hill, the great bare round hill that dominates north west Gower. Over the year (1838) he had lost *about twenty* of his sheep and lambs. The inexactness of his evidence suggests that he, like John Jenkins of Park-y-rhedyn, had a casual approach to his stock maintenance. Morgan Thomas, having taken some of these sheep, had sold them to a farmer in Llandewi, just two miles to the south of Landimore. But Joseph Gwyn had been sharp enough to detect that the Llandewi flock had sheep that bore his original marks. Morgan Thomas received for this crime a sentence of 15 months imprisonment in the house of correction at Cardiff with hard labour and the last week in each month in solitary confinement.

One of the more audacious cases was that in Neath, reported in August 1856. The practice had been to maintain the turf on the cricket pitch there by grazing sheep. This was too much temptation for one local who stole the sheep from off the pitch.

In September 1855 the Batcocks' case was presented at Quarter Sessions. Mr Tripp, for the prosecution and Mr Howard, for the defence, presented the evidence and the jury took no time in returning a verdict of 'guilty'. The chairman of the court then made an observation which, perhaps, tells us why the case had created such interest. He noted that the prisoners *had carried on one of the most systematic cases of sheep stealing he had ever remembered.* Assuming this supposition to be correct, Christopher had been stealing sheep for years. He had perfected a technique, it would appear, of bringing in more sheep than were his from the marsh and then, apparently, returning the surplus. But the surplus returned was apparent and not complete. Farmers like John Jenkins, with two to three hundred sheep on the marsh, were the perfect target. Jenkins was clearly very casual in his approach and may even have made some allowance for losses of this kind – perhaps that is why he was somewhat reluctant to prosecute. But William Thomas, who could ill-afford the loss of even one sheep, was far more astute and kept a close eye on his stock; in taking one of his sheep the Batcocks had made a great mistake.

Christopher's previous sentence had been one year for manslaughter but the heinous crime of sheep stealing attracted a stiffer sentence. Both men received two years imprisonment with the first two days of each month in solitary confinement.

If this sentence was meant to deter others from the same crime, it had little effect in the local vicinity. By 1855, such a crime had become a relative rarity but in the years following there were similar cases in north Gower. In November 1856 David Bowen, 'a very dirty and slovenly dressed middle aged man', was brought before the court. He lived in Bovehill, the higher hamlet of Landimore, a couple of miles west of Llanrhidian. He had made predations upon the sheep of John Bevan, a farmer who was also his neighbour. Following suspicions, a number of men had gathered to watch Bevan's sheep in the fields late at night and, sure enough, Bowen obliged them by stealing a sheep before their very eyes. When confronted by PS Jones the following morning he fell to his knees and begged forgiveness. In the courtroom the prisoner spoke simply in his own defence, 'All I can say is, it was poverty. I will never do so again, if I should be overlooked for this.' There followed a second charge from a Cheriton farmer and this sealed Bowen's fate. Even though he claimed, perhaps in truth, the sheep from Cheriton was already drowned when he took it, he was found guilty on both charges at Quarter Sessions and received four years penal servitude for each crime, both sentences running concurrently.

Reading his newspaper one morning in Sherborne, Charles Morgan noted with alarm that yet another case of sheep stealing had occurred; this time the culprit was William Beynon of Muzzard, a little farm some four miles west of Llanrhidian. Rather like Llanrhidian, there was a widespread practice of pasturing on the extensive common land available. Here, in West Gower, it was chiefly up on the hills. Any sheep left on these areas of common land were easy prey to someone minded to steal them. Bed-ridden old Philip Taylor of Glebe Farm, Cheriton, seemed an easy victim for small scale theft of this type but his son, who managed the farm, was capable and knowledgeable and was aware quite soon that sheep were going missing. As in Landimore, a number of men gathered to carry out the arrest and informal prosecution and William Beynon tried every means to mislead them. He claimed he had bought the sheep but off whom he did not know. He claimed they were taken in lieu of a debt owed him by Taylor but Taylor's son said there was no debt. He tried to wheedle all the arresting parties into some compromise that would evade justice but they did not want to know. He was in a panic about what his church companions and his wife would think. It was clear that she had no knowledge of what her husband was up to. Finally, after arguing in the garden of the local inn, 'The Britannia', he told the constable he would like to say goodbye to his victim, Philip Taylor. He went in and started whispering to the old man in his bed. 'We must go,' the constable admonished him. 'We might as well,' Beynon replied gloomily, 'because what I proposed to the old man he would not consent to.' He, too, received four years of penal servitude.

Chapter Seven

The Two Legged Fox

Business had been looking up at the Higher Mill in recent times; one of the witnesses at the sheep stealing case commented on the number of hands that had lately been employed by Christopher Batcock. But now, with his incarceration, the outlook would be bleak for Maria. She was, presumably, no miller herself, nor any kind of agricultural merchant or labourer. For ten years they had managed some form of livelihood whilst Christopher seemed rehabilitated in the community. Some of their late prosperity, it is true, may have derived from illegal activities including sheep stealing. Being a rector's daughter and having her mother living close by, it is unlikely that Christopher would have kept his wife fully informed of what he was up to. Maria now found herself without a proper source of income. Moreover, she is likely to have been the butt of much ill-feeling generated by her husband's nefarious activities; it is apparent that he had been stealing from his fellow parish councillors, John Jenkins and William Thomas for certain. There may have been many others who had suffered in similar ways.

To add to Maria's difficulties, we find that in 1856 her mother-in-law was also arraigned in court for failure to pay off debts which were incurred on the marriage of one of her daughters. Mr Howard, perhaps now a friend of the family, was again employed to defend a Batcock, this time against the demands of W. H. Hurndall, the well-known Swansea drapers, to whom was owed £5 11s 7d (£5.58). Mrs Batcock, described in the *Cambrian* as 'formerly of the Dolphin Inn', was presented as being in 'most unfortunate circumstances'. Her husband, Robert, was now nearing the end of his life and quite incapable of earning an income. At 73, he was becoming both blind and bed-ridden, a sorry spectacle. Being described in the *Cambrian* as 'formerly' of the Dolphin Inn, strongly suggests that that source of income was no longer available to them; the previous year the Batcocks had failed to secure a licence to sell liquor there. It is probable, therefore, that the Dolphin was no longer in the hands of the Batcocks at all. Mrs Batcock's debts derived from a 'very large debt incurred some three or four years since upon the intended marriage of one of the defendant's daughters'. If 'intended' means a marriage that never actually took place, this must refer to her daughter Maria who had died of consumption in 1855. We assume that it did not relate to the marriage of Louisa in distant Keswick in 1849. Even in that case, it is possible that money had to be laid out sufficiently to ensure that James Tregurtha would make an honest woman of Louisa. Although she had paid off £14 of this debt at one time, the balance remained outstanding. She was instructed to pay off the remaining debt at the rate of five shillings (25p) per month. Even this relatively small sum was an unwanted burden on a 'hard-pushed' family. James and Louisa came back to Swansea (Cross Street) at about the time Christopher and Francis were sent to prison. James worked as an engine fitter but, sadly, did not have long to live. Early in October (1856) he was taken ill with pneumonia and passed away on the 26th of the same month. This left Louisa with at least two children; Mansell and James (the latter born in 1852). In 1857, little James also died at the tender age of four. Within a month of his death, however, she had remarried to William Williams of Penclawdd and, within a year, had started a new family with him. In the light of later records it seems that she left her eldest son, Mansell, in the care of Maria and Christopher who had no children of their own.

Just a couple of months before the Batcocks' release in 1857, Charles Morgan died. For some years he had been a visitor to, rather than a resident of, the parish. He had maintained a lively interest in the affairs of the parish and took great delight in the *capital evidence* given by George Harris and company against the *impudent* Batcock. Only in his early sixties, his health had become somewhat variable although only weeks before his death he had taken a long walk across miles and miles of Dorset downland. His last entry in his diary told of his retiring to bed, feeling rather poorly. On April 5th he died, at Sherborne, of a fit – most likely a stroke.

Poor old Robert Batcock, 13 years Charles Morgan's senior, continued to decline and finally he died in 1859 – 'after a lapse of time, being both blind and bed-ridden'. This left what was once quite an extended family in a somewhat attenuated state.

It is likely that Mrs Batcock (senior) was living in the village, so too were her sons Christopher and Francis. Edward, as we have seen, had died some years previously – at sea. Louisa had also left home and was living in England with a man from the West Country. The death of six-year-old Maria Phelps at the Common (half a mile east of the village) in 1859 suggests that Christopher's brother-in-law, John Phelps, was still in the area although also, apparently, present at Aberavon as an iron-monger. The overbearing presence of the Batcock family in the community was, however, much diminished from former times. Christopher's stock in the village must have been at a very low ebb; as a known felon who had stolen from the very partners he worked with in the parish council – he was not a man to be trusted. In spite of this, after his release in 1857, the parish council continued to be held in his presence at the Dolphin Inn.

Since Christopher had emerged from prison, the harvests had been fair with reasonable weather. But 1860 was a miserable year. Cold and wet, the harvests were in question from the start. Haymaking was fair but there was much sickness and mortality among sheep and fodder was in short supply. Hard times were back again.

To meet Christopher Batcock, at dead of night in a quiet and lonely spot could still, in spite of the punishments meted out to him, be an intimidating experience. Presumably that is why, on the night of the 26th April, 1860, William Jones did not engage Christopher in conversation. It all happened in a field at Leason, which is a hamlet just a mile to the west of Llanrhidian village. The houses there were grouped round two main farms, one belonging to John Dunn at the west end of the hamlet and the other belonging to Samuel Jones – right in the heart of the hamlet. Samuel worked his farm with his sons George and

William. William, the younger son, was 27 at the time. What he was doing in the fields at gone 11 o'clock at night, we do not know. Neither does his account explain how it was that he was able to recognise Christopher Batcock in the dark, far away from any lighted buildings. In fact, the accounts surrounding these events, as reported in the *Cambrian* newspaper, are riddled with inconsistencies. It is clear, however, that William saw Christopher Batcock with another person on his father's lands at Leason. Who the other person was, we are not told. William intimated that he knew who it was, but that name was never raised in court. The two characters were followed until they were near the farm buildings. William secreted himself opposite the cow-house of the farm. Shortly, the two men walked up the lane having left a cart some way behind them. As they passed the hidden man a cock crew from the cow-house opposite. Batcock, being now somewhat deaf, probably did not hear this but his companion told him that there were fowls in

Buildings of Samuel Jones's farm at Leason.

the cow-house. "Let's go in," said Batcock. William Jones saw them go in and, shortly, heard a great deal of clucking, squawking and beating of wings. They came out with two fowls which appeared to be injured because he could trace their subsequent route from blood stains. The two men made their way off across the fields towards Llanrhidian.

A little later that night, about one o'clock in the morning, Batcock's cart was observed moving along a village lane. The cart was driven by Christopher's nephew who, we may speculate, was the figure accompanying him earlier. Who was this nephew? There are two candidates, on the basis of the records we have to hand. It may have been Thomas George Phelps, the son of John and Jane Phelps. Thomas would have been just short of his fourteenth birthday at the time of these events but we cannot be certain that he was living in the village at the time. More likely, however, is that the nephew was Louisa Batcock's son, James Tregurtha. He was the same age as Thomas and surely, as a kind of adopted son, accompanied Christopher in much of his work. The local policeman of the time, PC John Shore, stopped and searched the cart but apparently found nothing. It may have been that this search was a result of his already having been alerted to nefarious goings-on in the village by William Jones.

PC John Shore (number 54 in the constabulary) probably led a quiet life in rural Gower but seems to have reacted with some promptitude to William Jones's complaints. The facts of the case were explained to him and he immediately connected them with a complaint made the previous week by Henry Willis, the miller of Stackpool Mill near Fairyhill in Reynoldston. The previous Friday he had a hen and seven chickens of a distinctive breed and very recognisable marking. He had fed them in the evening but the next morning they were all gone. Willis told John Shore about this. On the 27th April, with fresh evidence to pursue, John Shore obtained a search warrant 'under the hand and seal of Starling Benson' and immediately went to the Higher Mill. Starling Benson was a very significant figure in Swansea and, as a resident of Fairyhill House in Reynoldston parish, was a neighbour to the Willis's of Stackpool Mill. Maria answered the door, any commotion that occurred then was unheard by the deaf and sleeping Batcock who was in an adjacent downstairs room. Christopher was roused and John Shore charged him with the theft of the chicken. Out of the corner of his eye, Shore spotted Maria going upstairs *rather hastily*. Her complicity at this stage tells us all we need to know about her knowledge of her husband's activities. Shore saw her throw a towel over a basket of five fowls ready-dressed to go to market. These he took into 'police custody'. He then went outside and found, running around the mill garden, seven chickens which he also took into custody. Then a peculiar incident took place – Maria caught hold of two of the chickens and, according to PC Shore, plucked the feathers from their heads. He asked what she was doing, "Only stroking them," Maria answered. These seven chicken were later presented to Henry Willis who had no trouble identifying them as his own. When Shore asked Batcock where he got the chicken from he could elicit no reply, so the policeman told him that they were Willis's chicken from Stackpool. "I can hatch chickens as well as Thomas Willis," said Batcock. (Thomas was Henry Willis's uncle and the owner of the Stackpool Mill.)

A cart was fetched and the little party of PC Shore, Christopher Batcock and Samuel Jones prepared to make the journey into Swansea which would lead to Batcock's incarceration. We are told that Samuel Jones and John Shore got out of the cart to walk up a steep hill. It is likely that this was the hill leading directly up from the village green in Llanrhidian since there are no other steep hills in that direction towards Swansea. Shore turned round and saw that Batcock, alone in the cart, was bleeding. He asked him what the matter was and realised that Christopher had attempted to take his own life by cutting his throat. In Christopher's left hand waistcoat pocket, Shore found a long-bladed, sprung, folding knife with which the deed was done. In other circumstances, Batcock's life might have been in danger from blood loss, if nothing else. Conveyed swiftly to Swansea gaol, however, he received excellent attention from the prison surgeon, Mr Hancorne. His wound, chiefly under his left ear, was stitched and he was committed to the infirmary. Much the same as would happen today, he was watched 'night and day' lest he should try again to harm

Her Majesty's Prison at Swansea during reconstruction, just before the time of Christopher Batcock's incarceration.
(Photograph courtesy of the City and County Swansea: Swansea Museum).

himself. Within a couple of days the surgeon noted that he was doing well with no 'unfavourable symptons'. He was being cared for in a brand new building completed just a year previously – the same building (in essence) as is standing on the site in Swansea today.

This attempt on his own life is one of the few insights into Christopher's own mentality and personality. His departure from the village on this occasion must have caused him great despondency. Not only had he been caught in yet another crime against fellow villagers but their evident hostility to him would have lent to him a sense of great alienation – less bearable in an old, rural and static community of the 19th century than it would be today. Moreover, he was leaving his wife in a decrepit mill with no visible means of support. His ageing mother, perhaps now the only other remaining member of the family in the area was also in precarious circumstances as regards income. His sense of self-worth could not have been lower. We also see in this suicidal act the volatility of a man given to strong emotional reactions. And yet he may have concealed the strength of his emotions from his enforced companions on that day so that, when the moment came, he could carry out his attempted suicide. John Shore was heavily censured for his failure to check the prisoner for items that might be capable of causing harm but it may have been Christopher's deliberately calm manner that persuaded him that a search was not needed.

Batcock's case was to come before the court on Friday, May 11th. Once again, this was clearly quite an occasion. Not only would large numbers of local people have turned out to attend the hearing but also Swansea folk who looked to these occasions as potential entertainment. Adding to that entertainment and the colour of the occasion would have been the sight and sound of animal exhibits – some of the chicken in question were present, either in the courtroom or just outside. Their quiet clucking in wicker containers, would raise expectation of interesting developments.

Two charges of stealing chickens were laid against Christopher Batcock. The court heard first the crime alleged to have been committed on the earlier date, so the theft of chicken from Stackpool Mill was brought in. Henry Willis took the stand and told how he had attended his birds on the night of the 20th April but found seven of them missing the following morning. He was quite particular about their description; six of them had 'top knots' and one had a most 'peculiar whiteness about the bill'. Of course, Maria had done her best to remove some of these characteristics before all the birds had been taken in to custody. Then, to the amusement of onlookers, the birds were produced in court for general inspection. Henry Willis was absolutely convinced that these were his birds. His uncle (Thomas Willis), with whom he resided, also took the stand and affirmed the identity of the birds.

The *Cambrian* newspaper, on which we rely for the detail of this case, is inclined to be a little woolly in style on this occasion. Some of the dates quoted are contradictory and the detail of events could be clearer. Also, it was the paper's style not to recount the questions asked in court but only the answers. Therefore we have to infer from the answers given what the line of defence was that was taken by Batcock's counsel – Mr Simons of Merthyr. Initially, Mr Simons seemed to take the line that the fowls could not be clearly identified as those missing. He then began to suggest that there were more reasons for birds to go missing than laying the cause at the feet of a rogue miller. Was the door of the hen house shut? Had fowls ever gone missing on previous occasions? Were there any foxes in the neighbourhood? Thomas Willis said that he *did not know that there were any foxes in the neighbourhood, except two-legged foxes*. This comment was greeted with laughter throughout the court – the public were, indeed, being well entertained that day. Thomas Willis was quite correct in saying that foxes were not a problem in Gower. Charles Morgan, in his diary, relates how the local hunt (a pastime for which he had no taste) was supplied with a bag fox because of the lack of local vermin. It may be that Mr Simons, from Merthyr, had assumed that Gower was not short of foxes and that this as a reasonable line of defence. In the event, he still submitted that the case was not strong enough against his client to secure a conviction; the mere occurrence of stolen property on his premises did not mean that he was the thief.

The case may, therefore, have been in the balance when the second charge was brought against him of stealing chicken from William Jones of Leason. William's evidence was of a clear nature and, if he was believed, pointed directly at Christopher as a thief. He told the events of the night he had seen Christopher and his accomplice on his father's land. Who the accomplice was remained a mystery. If it was Mansel Tregurtha, it may have been thought that he was too young to be dragged into his uncle's criminal activities. The two cases, taken together, suggested too strongly that Christopher was indeed stealing chickens from his neighbours and the whole case was committed to quarter sessions in July.

Incarcerated in Swansea gaol for three months before his trial, Christopher was in sore need of some communication with his wife. He could read and write and he found a

Llwyn Madog in the hills near Builth Wells, a different world from industrial Glamorgan.

sympathetic prison warder to supply him with paper and pencil so that he could maintain a correspondence with Maria. This went on for some weeks and would have had little significance had it not been that it was clandestine. The warder, Evan Morgan, chose not to tell his superiors what was going on. Suspicions grew, however, and on the 27th June, Christopher was confronted with those suspicions. He confirmed that Morgan *had often taken out and brought in secret correspondence in the shape of letters etc* to and from Maria. Evan Morgan was 'diswiped' from the service as a result of this lack of observance of prison rules.

Finally, on the 6th July, Christopher Batcock's case came before quarter sessions in Swansea's old town hall. Presiding on that day was Mr Henry Thomas, the chair of the Glamorgan Sessions. Nine times a year he sallied out from his quiet mountain retreat (Llwyn Madog, in the hills above Beulah near Builth Wells) to hear the misdemeanours of the industrial south. He probably felt more at home as he heard the details of

Batcock's case; a very rural case compared with the pimping and crimping on Swansea's mean streets. Once again, the *Cambrian* account serves to confuse as much as illuminate – it states that the fowls stolen were the property of 'John Willis of Llanrhidian'. This does not tally with any other known facts although it is interesting that the Lower Mill in Llanrhidian was in the possession of the Willis family through much of the 20th century. It would, however, seem a brazen act had Christopher stolen such distinctive birds from a near neighbour and then left them run round his garden in the heart of the village. Stackpool Mill, the presumed site of the theft was some three miles away to the west; a more comfortable distance from which to steal.

The facts of the case were laid out before Henry Thomas, the witnesses reiterated their stories. It was pointed out that Christopher did not deny the charge made against him by PC John Shore. Not only was Christopher Batcock found guilty but his former conviction for sheep stealing was raised in consideration of the sentence. Henry Thomas, by many accounts a fair and 'social' man, gave a harsh sentence, four years of penal servitude.

Chapter Eight

Spare the Vanquished

England and Wales, by 1860, had gone through a period of agrarian unrest and an increase in criminal activity that had given the authorities grave concern about the manageability of the newly enfranchised masses. Many politicians sought, through enlightened law-making, to reduce the ills that caused unrest. Underlying their work was a belief in the natural nobility of the human spirit that could be cultivated in the appropriate political and cultural environment. Others looked for ways to 'contain' the unrest and law breaking that accompanied the new enfranchisement of the masses. Mixed in with their views was an opinion of the moral degeneracy of the working class and the need to address its natural bent towards

106

idleness and crime. The response of the judiciary and the penal system to the new demands being made on them was coloured by the sentiments and theories of both parties. For example, prison buildings were both improved and increased in number. There was much debate as to the efficacy of systems within the prisons and much of this debate centred on what experts considered to be the mainsprings of the criminal nature. Faced with international organised crime, drug and people trafficking and large scale anti-social behaviour, the system of that day would have appeared woefully, if not ludicrously, inadequate. Faced, however, with a stolen hen here, the theft of a sheep there and the regular incidence of pick-pocketing on the streets of Swansea, the debate appears to take on a more reasonable sense of proportion. The Reverend John Burt, who was, for a period, the assistant chaplain of Pentonville Prison (to which Christopher Batcock was first sent in 1860) held a strong belief that separation was the key to 'attacking' the criminal character. He wrote, 'The passions of the criminal by which he is chiefly activated, are usually excessive and malignant. Penal discipline finds the will vigorous, but vicious, propelled powerfully, but lawlessly. It is this vicious activity that is subjugated by protracted seclusion and wholesome discipline . . . The will is . . . subdued . . . bent or broken and the moral character is made plastic . . . The will is bent in its direction, it is broken in its resistance to virtue, its vicious activity is suppressed only to leave it open to the control of better motives.' (As quoted by Sean McConville, in *The Oxford History of the Prison*, ed. Morris and Rothman, 1995.)

Penal servitude was, therefore, an approach inspired not only by a belief in the viciousness and degeneracy of the criminal character but also by a belief in its ability to be reformed. In practice, it constituted a nine month period of 'separation'

followed by the balance of the sentence being completed in a
public works prison. The principle of 'separation' was that, left
alone and without the malign influence of others, the criminal
would reflect on his ways and consider the re-routing of his life.
In the public works prison he would be subjugated to 'wholesome discipline' through regular and protracted toil. Older
prisoners might avoid heavy manual work and be given duties
relating to prison maintenance. Clothing was deliberately
uncomfortable and meant to remind the prisoner of his abject
position. All items of clothing were marked with the broad
arrow that signified his incarceration. Hair was rough cut to a
'convict's crop', facial hair removed with clippers to a rough
stubble. In spite of this harsh regime there was also the
possibility that the prisoner's sentence might be reduced by
good behaviour and positive compliance with the aims of penal
servitude. If the prison authorities thought that 'the will was
broken in its resistance to virtue' then an early release could be
considered. Unfortunately, it was more likely that the prisoner's
health was broken rather than his will. It is likely that the state
of health of many convicts was poor on entering prison and
continued to deteriorate within the walls.

On the day following his conviction, the 7th July, Christopher
was seen by the prison chaplain. From then on he began his
nine month period of separation. The prison 'Return' was
completed and signed by William Cox, governor of Swansea
Gaol, on the 4th September – the date that Batcock was moved
on. Cox gives us, for the first time, a description of the man.
Christopher Batcock was described as 'square' but of erect
bearing. His height was five feet and eight inches, rather short
by today's average. His complexion was 'rather sallow', his hair
brown and eyes grey. Of distinguishing marks about the face it
was noted that his forehead was receding and that he was of

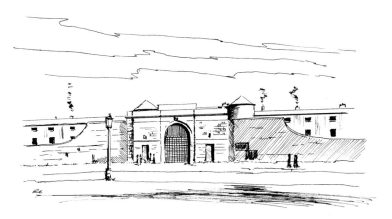

The grim entrance to Millbank Prison.

'full eye'. Above his left eye was a long scar suggestive of adventures that have evaded this record. He was described as 'rather deaf'. And then a little insight; his 'excitable manner' was noted. Whilst he was at Swansea Gaol his character was described as 'sullen and resolute' although his conduct was orderly. One senses a man filled with anger and resentment.

After two months in Swansea Gaol, the time came for Christopher to be moved on. On September 4th he was transported, presumably by rail, to London. If nothing else, this would have been a novel experience to a man who had never travelled outside South Wales. By the evening he would have reached London and was taken to Millbank Prison, on whose site the present Tate Gallery now stands. Entering the 'Reception Ward' he might have been awed by the lofty, cathedral like height of the building with endless cells stretching away for the solitary confinement of prisoners. On arrival at the prison, Batcock would have been stripped, washed and examined for signs of disease.

Crude and forbidding now as then, the entrance to Dartmoor Prison.

Directed to his cell, his hair would have been cut and the prison rules read out to him as they would be for every succeeding week of his stay. Millbank was kept scrupulously clean and had a reputation, according to Charles Dickens at least, for the severity of its regime. It was well that Christopher was only staying there for 23 days. No other prison in London, possibly in Britain, had such a poor reputation for health. Built on low-lying, marshy ground it had an appalling death rate of nearly seven percent per annum. Every year there were nearly 12,000 cases of illness in the prison. When one considers that only 2,700 prisoners a year (1854 figures) passed through its portals that is an alarming figure. Illness was 10 times more rife in Millbank than in the prison hulks of the Thames. Millbank was a kind of clearing house for convict prisoners from all over England and Wales. After a period of consideration, prisoners were passed on to other prisons such as Pentonville, Parkhurst and Dartmoor. The bulk of male prisoners went to Pentonville; the governor at Millbank believed that he 'kept Pentonville up'. And so it was with Christopher Batcock who, on the 27th September, was transferred there.

Like Millbank, Pentonville in north London was built on the 'panopticon' principle. Five wings radiated like spokes of a masonry wheel with the intention that staff could see and control prisoners from a central point. It had been built between 1840 and 1842 for the express purpose of holding convict prisoners like Batcock under the 'separate' system. Each cell was 13 feet long, 7 feet wide and 9 feet high. Prisoners were engaged in work such as picking coir (a tarred rope) or weaving. Christopher had already begun weaving in his short stay in Millbank having been fortunate in escaping the more ubiquitous and unpopular tailoring. As a weaver he was noted as being 'fairly industrious' and his progress in training was described as '1st class'. Throughout his period in Pentonville his conduct was 'fairly good' – a reserved descriptor. He remained sullen and resolute, a man grimly persevering in adversity.

After four months and a day in Pentonville, and having endured one of the coldest Christmases ever recorded, Christopher had completed the nine months of separation that constituted the first part of a penal servitude sentence (his months in Swansea gaol had also been in separation and made up the 'balance'). A decision had to be made as to the prison where he would complete the rest of his sentence. Usual practice was to send prisoners on to a 'public works' prison where heavy labour was required for activities such as building docks in Portsmouth, Gibraltar or Chatham, or to institutions where the degree of human strength required was less. In view of his age, state of health and the general prevailing practice, it

Convicts going to labour.
(Picture courtesy of the Dartmoor Prison Heritage Centre).

was almost inevitable that he would be sent to Dartmoor. In the middle of winter, January 28th, 1861, prisoner number 6038, Christopher Long Batcock began the two-day journey that would take him to the heart of Devon's wild moors. As the sun set across the bleak, cold moors, he would have entered the prison beneath the crude archway marked with the simple Latin inscription 'Parcere Subjectis' – Spare the Vanquished. On arrival his poor state of health was implied by the term 'invalid' being attached to him. When he had entered the prison system 18 months earlier his health, in spite of his self-inflicted wound, was described as good. Millbank and Pentonville had done him no favours in this respect. In fact, the majority of convicts sent to Dartmoor were described as invalid at this time. On account of its 'bracing' air Dartmoor was seen as an opportunity for convicts to recuperate before taking up the onerous weight of public works. That first winter on Dartmoor was a severe one but, fortunately for Christopher, that was probably the worst weather he experienced there.

Although we would consider the duties performed in Dart-moor as irksome, tedious and demanding, by the standards of the prison system of the time those duties were considered to be relatively undemanding. Even so, we understand that some prisoners went to extraordinary lengths to maintain their invalid status so that they could avoid being pressed into hard labour. Ground glass, soda, soap, even pins might be consumed to achieve this effect, sometimes with fatal results. Another advantage of invalid status was that accommodation was in the more comfortable invalid ward with a hammock for a bed. The alternative was a cast iron cell with little or no ventilation and a hard bed. In the 1860's the prison regime was particularly harsh; convicts would rise at 5.00am and after breakfast and a brief religious service would work from 7.00 to 11.10. After a long dinner break they would work through to 5.15 when they

Hard labour in the prison quarry.
(Picture courtesy of the Dartmoor Prison Heritage Centre).

would return to cells for supper. In the evening they could attend education sessions or read books. By 7.55 all prisoners would be in cells and lights out. Food, in theory, was basic but wholesome. In reality it had a very poor reputation; complaints were made of rotten potatoes, stinking meat, insects in the bread and so on. Given the nature of their duties and the cold wet climate, prisoners were ill-equipped by their diet to improve in health. Even the warders found conditions difficult; it is told that, in the 1850's, one warder resigned on arrival at the prison declaring that he would not do one hour's duty in such a place.

Christopher Batcock did not manage to get into his weaving practice at Dartmoor; that trade was not available there. His prison trade was described as 'tailor' and this would involve, principally, making clothes for prison warders and the metropolitan police force. To what extent his invalid status kept him from this trade we do not know but the surgeon designated him as 'invalid' through the first three quarters of 1861. All this time his behaviour was described as either 'good' or 'very good'. At the end of his stay in Dartmoor his general character and conduct were described as 'exemplary'. He was one of the older prisoners at Dartmoor and might have been rather lonely. He may, however, have found a comradely fellow Welshman in John Williams who was convicted in Swansea Gaol, on the same day as Christopher, for stealing candlesticks and smock frocks. Although from Merthyr, he appeared to have been operating in the Neath area. John served his 'separation' months in Swansea and Millbank (the latter for more than five months) and was then sent straight to Dartmoor the month after Christopher arrived there. He was a rough looking man: short, swarthy, an upper tooth missing and a broken nose with a blue spot on his right cheek. But, if the two got together, they would surely have reminisced about the homeland and about their past lives.

By the fourth quarter of 1861 Christopher was no longer being classed as an invalid and conditions, as well as work would have become much harder for him. Through the winter months of 1862 he laboured on and into the summer but his health would not hold up against this great physical strain. John Williams, too, must have been struggling. After his months in Millbank, that terrible place would have taken a toll on his health. By the summer of 1862 he was definitely not coping with the supposed healthy climate of Dartmoor.

The bad health of prisoners throughout the kingdom was clearly creating difficulties in any attempt to run the prison system in a remotely humane way. Rather than reviewing the efficacy of prison regimes it seems that a solution was seen to be the erection of purpose-built infirmary prisons. With this function in mind, the Woking Invalid Convict Prison (in Surrey) came into existence in 1859. John Williams was sent there in July of 1862 and would have met dozens of ex-Dartmoor men there, all with their health wrecked by that place. When he left Dartmoor he probably expressed a wish that he would see Christopher follow him. Within two months that wish would have been fulfilled; Christopher left Dartmoor on the 15th September to arrive in Woking the following day.

Dartmoor, with its wild hills and wet climate, may not have seemed so very different from his native Wales but the dry heathlands and neat villages of Surrey would have appeared a foreign country to Christopher. These he would only have seen in transit before the prison doors closed once again on him on the 16th September. Receiving immediate medical assessment, the surgeon's report declared Batcock to be 'delicate'. Although this was a standard descriptor of the service it does sound rather

Dartmoor prison amongst the high moors.
(Picture courtesy of the Dartmoor Prison Heritage Centre).

euphemistic whilst suggesting that the subject deserved careful management at the very least. Christopher would have reacquainted himself with old John Williams, now 58 years old, and this would have made conditions seem easier. The climate, too, would have been much more agreeable. As the Mediterranean climate would seem to a person from south-east England so, too, would the climate of dry, warm Surrey to a man from Wales. Conditions in the gaol were, as one might expect, somewhat easier than had been the case in Dartmoor. In fact, there may have been concerns that the regime was too lenient. In 1869, the governor of the Woking Invalid Prison was the victim of a stabbing incident and the case came to trial. In the course of the case, evidence was given as to the prisoners' diet which was considered to be very generous. Victorian sensibilities were inflamed to hear that steaks, chops and jellies among other delicacies were being served up to the inmates. The suggestion being made was that the conditions were so easy there as to make an attack on the governor or his subordinates more, rather than less, likely.

At first, all went well and Christopher's behaviour was 'very good', but in the winter months of the following year his behaviour deteriorated. Whether this was a general deterioration or as a result on one or two incidents, we do not know. The surgeon reported him now as 'rather delicate', perhaps a slight improvement in health. He was now 47 years old and more than half way through his sentence. Any remission to be gained on that sentence needed awards for good behaviour and it is not surprising to find Christopher returning to 'very good' descriptors of his behaviour in the spring and summer months. His health, however, deteriorated and by the autumn he was once again 'delicate'. Perhaps in view of his deteriorating health but also in recognition of his generally very good conduct and behaviour, Batcock was now awarded an early release. On 10th October, 1863, Christopher Long Batcock became an ordinary civilian once more and the doors of Woking Infirmary Prison were opened to him.

Chapter Nine

Based on 'Hard Times'
by Hubert von Herkomer

Stepping Out

On a day in early October, perhaps with late summer's warmth in the balmy Surrey air or the first blasts of winter blowing the leaves off the trees, Christopher Batcock stepped out of Woking Infirmary Prison, a free man. Two hundred miles from home, what was he to do? His licence papers tell us that his destination was Reigate, a mellow, red-bricked Surrey town beneath the North Downs some 18 miles to the east. Why should he be going to Reigate? The author would be deceiving his readers if he did not make clear, at this point, that Christopher Batcock seems to have stepped out of the pages of history – no further record can be found of him. In speculating on his next and following moves, however, some strange facts (or rather absences of facts) come to light. So, it seems worthwhile to proceed with the story just a little longer, if only in speculation.

Although a free man on that day in October, he was not a well man. Poor of hearing and weak in health, his next move was indeed problematic. It was a mild autumn but one with many gales. The destination of Reigate is hard to explain. Did he have friends or relatives there or was there some other connection? The name 'Batcock', particularly when spelt with a 't' rather than a 'd', is sufficiently uncommon to make searches worthwhile. At the time of the events recorded in this account, 'Batcocks' were to be found in only a few localities outside London. The Gower peninsula was one of the chief of those localities, another was around Bristol. A notable cluster occurred in and around the little village of Shere in Surrey. It is an odd coincidence that, on his journey to Reigate, Christopher would very likely have passed through Shere, carrying on through Dorking before arriving in Reigate. In the 1861 census there was even a 'Batcock' family to be found in Reigate itself, or rather just outside in the village of Horley. Here John Batcock, his wife and mother lived, but they were born and bred in Surrey and had no obvious connection with Christopher. It is likely, then, that Batcock's purpose in making his way to Reigate was for reasons other than connecting with some member of the family. In his fragile state of health he might have made his way to the local workhouse under direction of the prison in Woking although they might have directed him to some place much nearer – such as Guildford or Dorking. The records for the Reigate Workhouse have, sadly, been altogether lost, so this can be neither proved nor disproved. Workhouses at towns between Woking and Reigate have no record of Christopher Batcock being admitted through their door.

The demure Surrey town of Reigate, a world away from industrial South Wales or the wild Gower landscape.

Young convicts in Millbank Prison were sometimes sent to an institution in Reigate known as the Philanthropic Farm School of Redhill (a growing suburb of Reigate). This was often on the basis of a conditional pardon being granted in the expectation that a reformation programme would be completed at Redhill. It was a well established school aimed at the reform and rehabilitation of young criminals. Most of the young inmates were encouraged, at the end of their term in the school, to emigrate; in the 1860's this appears to have been predominantly to Canada. Life in the school centred chiefly on the farm. In October 1863, the farm's flock of sheep was being built up, 80 were purchased early in the month. Having some experience with sheep, albeit in a largely illegal way, did Christopher offer some 'expertise' to the institution? The Philanthropic School was clearly linked into the prison system of the day and the possibility exists that Christopher Batcock was sent there from Woking as a means of restoring his financial position and his health through some gentle labour at the place. Presumably, this would have been a short term solution to his problems but may have been seen as part of a rehabilitation process by the prison system itself. Unfortunately, among the substantial records of the school, there is no mention of Christopher nor any indication as to whether casual employment, of the type suggested here, took place.

And what lay beyond Reigate? If we knew the whereabouts of his wife, Maria, we would be better placed to guess at his next movements. Within a year of Christopher's incarceration we find (through the census) Maria established in the bustling heart of Llanelli. Just a little over a mile away, across the estuary from Llanrhidian, but many miles' journey by toilsome roads, Llanelli had been an everyday visual presence for Maria with its smoking factory chimneys and bustling port. So, when faced with the dilemma of what to do after Christopher was taken off to London, the smoke across the water spoke to her of opportunities ahead. With her, she took young Mansel Tregurtha, her nephew, and set up as a greengrocer in Thomas Street, a strong retailing position in the heart of what was then just a little town. The Census return suggests that her shop was at number 35, next to the long disappeared 'Farmers Arms'. Although there were about six other public houses in the immediate vicinity, this was no mean, 'down-town' location. Close by was the parish church with its venerable market cross; around this were handsome town houses reflecting considerable wealth. Whilst requiring little in the way of skill, her new trade and excellent location must surely have required some capital. Had this been acquired through the sale of effects at the mill? One imagines that she needed rather more capital than this was likely to raise and there may have been some support through her family, one of her brothers perhaps.

Maria Batcock's shop in Thomas Street, Llanelli – centre of picture.

This is where the story becomes even more difficult to follow. Even with the amazing access to census, birth, marriage and death records that today's technology places at our fingertips, it has proved impossible to locate the further whereabouts of any of the key players in the story. When Christopher was 'sent down' in 1860, his mother would have been a venerable 72 years old. There is, however, no record of her demise to be found. Of his brothers, only one may have been still surviving – Francis, Christopher's accomplice sheep stealer in 1855. With regard to Francis, there are records of a Francis Batcock living in Oystermouth, Swansea's seaside suburb, but these do not seem to relate to the Llanrhidian Francis. Another Francis Batcock at the time was a seafarer and yet another came from farming stock in the little village of Cheriton, further west. Christopher's sisters had all passed on or disappeared from the record before the events of 1860. His brothers-in-law, John or Robert Phelps, who might have been assisting their sister Maria to set up shop in Llanelli, are similarly absent from the record although Jane Phelps and her son Thomas are to be found in Oystermouth in 1861. Thomas continues to be present on the record throughout the rest of the century as a worker at various trades in Swansea. Christopher's other nephew, Mansell Tregurtha, son of Louisa Batcock, also vanishes from the records. Louisa, as has been noted, had remarried in 1857 and gone to start a new family in Penclawdd. She was present in the 1861 census, living in Rodney Street in Swansea, but not in the 1871 census. Louisa Williams is not an unusual name but a record of Louisa Williams's death in Gower, in 1865, may well relate to her. Her husband stayed on with their little daughter, Fanny Louisa Williams.

Twenty years earlier, Christopher had a new sister-in-law in the form of Susan Cornish, the servant in Cae Forgan who had been compromised by Robert Batcock. On his death, in 1846, Susan had eventually returned home to Suffolk. She lived in Bury St Edmunds (44 Risbygate Street) to the grand old age of 84. She lies buried in the town cemetery together with some of her long-lived brothers and sisters. Her family were doing well in the foundry business and provision was made for her by a caring brother so that she should not enter penury. She never remarried. One wonders what memories flooded back to her, in her latter days, of life, back in Gower, the children she cared for and the wild Batcock family whose name she bore. When she left the service of the Morgans, her place was taken by her sister, Caroline Cornish. This seems to have been a successful employment but, eventually, Caroline left the Morgan's service to marry, in 1848, a local man called William Lloyd from neighbouring Cillibion. The newly married couple then moved into Pwllybrag where Caroline, in the 1851 census, professed her

East Anglian trade of 'straw bonnet maker'. She successfully raised a family and lived to the same grand age as her sister. She died at Pwllybrag in 1906 having outlived her husband by 15 years. With her, too, died some of the last memories of those days in the middle of the 19th century when the Batcock name was so well known to the village.

We presume that Maria and Christopher had maintained some contact throughout his imprisonment. Christopher would surely have known of his wife's business venture in Llanelli and one would imagine that, between them, they might have tried to find the means for him to come to Llanelli. Or, perhaps, it may have seemed a duty to Maria to join her husband for an uncertain future in England. On the other hand she may have indicated to him her desire for a separation in consideration of the difficulties into which his criminal activities had led her. Whatever choice she made, she was not living in Llanelli in 1871, nor is she to be found in any record that this writer has seen after 1861. There is a teasing record of a death of 'Hannah Maria Badcock' in Fulham, London, in 1878. The age of this woman was about right to match records of 'Anna Maria' and one can image an anxious Londoner adding the 'H' to 'Anna' for the benefit of the recorder. But this is rather tenuous for proper consideration. It is not improbable, however, that Anna Maria, if she left Llanelli to go to England on her husband's release, may have ended up in London.

Whatever may have happened, the decamping of the Batcock clan away from Llanrhidian and, apparently, from the Swansea region did take place. The Batcocks who were in the village in 1860 must have felt, each of them, *persona non grata*, any place was better than home. And yet the success with which they seem to have disappeared from the official record is particularly striking. Neither in census records nor records of deaths are they to be found; unless some extraordinary and selective catastrophe struck them all down, it seems that they entered a substratum of society that evaded the official record. Histories of the period suggest that a vast army of vagrants was on the move across Britain at this time. As one writer (T. A. Critchley, *A History of the Police in England and Wales 900-1966*) puts it, 'A vast army of tramps, thugs, poachers and swindlers begged, or peddled or thieved their way from one market town to another . . .'. For Christopher, vagrancy is a very likely outcome, but a dangerous one for a man whose health had been crippled by an overbearing prison system. In his state of health and penury it is hard to imagine that he could survive for long. Perhaps, one morning, some country labourer found a stiff and motionless body huddled under a Surrey hedge by the roadside. Perhaps in some town or city of the south of England, this son of Gower met his end –

'Batcock's Stile' – the only memorial to the 'Two Legged Fox'.

destitute, homeless and hopeless. And, perhaps, clutched in his hand or hidden in his rough coat, may have been some letters from Maria that might have given him identity. The two legged fox had left the pages of history.

Postscript

A hundred years after these events, a young man stepped out from Reigate. He was making his way into a teaching career through training in South Wales, probation in the English Midlands and finally to residence in Gower. He taught in Swansea for 31 years. Little did that young man think that he would take an interest in a felonious fox that would lead him back, 40 years later, to the town from which he started.

Appendix

Transcripts from the *Cambrian* newspaper.

Readers may be interested in the exact text of the reports in the *Cambrian* newspaper. These contain details which, for the sake of maintaining some narrative flow, may have been omitted from the main text of the book. It will also be noted that a degree of interpretation by the author has taken place. Readers may well, after reading these transcripts, consider that the truth of the matter is not as represented by the author. I hope that the provision of this appendix will assist them to make up their own mind!

TIMBER THEFT
Cambrian 1.7.1843.
Robert Batcock was charged with having stolen a quantity of timber, the property of the Rev. H. K. James of Llanrhidian – Rev. H. K. James was examined by Mr. T. Attwood and stated that in June last he was engaged in building a schoolhouse in the parish of Llanrhidian and had a piece of timber about 23 feet long near the building which was missed on the 11th of June – Mr. Tripp who defended the prisoner, cross examined Mr. James who said that the schoolroom was built by subscription, but that the timber was bought by himself, and paid for with his own money, and did not belong to the subscribers. Mr. Attwood re-examined the witness, but nothing was elicited. Mr. Tripp made an objection to the indictment and contended

that the property was not properly described as it belonged to the subscribers as joint tenants and not to Mr. James. The court overruled the objection. A workman, in the prosecutor's employ, proved that the timber was missed on the day in question. Mr. George Gordon, constable, Llanrhidian, stated that he went to a mill belonging to the prisoner and found the five pieces of timber produced. Prisoner said at the time that he did not steal them, he stated that he had cut them to make door frames. – William Davi.. carpenter, who was engaged in the building, proved that the timber found at the prisoner's mill was the same as that missed. The chairman then summed up the evidence, remarking that one point very unfavourable to the prisoner was his having made use of the timber, even supposing it had not been taken by him. The Chairman at the same time remarked that they could not safely convict the prisoner as the timber was not properly identified. The jury accordingly acquitted the prisoner. The Chairman, addressing the prisoner, told him he had a very narrow escape and expressed a hope he would take it as a warning for the future.

VIOLENT ASSAULT ON PHILIP MORRIS
Cambrian 15.6.1844.
Swansea Petty Sessions
At these Sessions, held at our Townhall on Tuesday before the Revs. Dr. Hewson and J. Collins, John Grove and J. H. Smith, Esqrs. – Edward and Christopher Badcock, two brothers, of the parish of Llanrhidian, appeared pursuant to a warrant charging them with having violently assaulted Phillip Morris, also of the parish of Llanrhidian. By the evidence of the complainant who appeared with several prominent marks of violence about the mouth, cycs, &c., it appeared that a scandalous report, which affected his character, was current in the village, which, he was

informed, had been given currency to by one of the defendants. He therefore called at his parents' house to remonstrate with him, but he was not at home. He subsequently met him in a lane near the village, and asked him how he gave out such a report. The defendant denied that he had, and immediately afterwards used some threat, knocked him down, then repeated the blow, and kicked him violently about the body. His brother, the other defendant, then came up and used great violence towards him. He (complainant) became quite insensible, and when recovered, found that he had been moved some yards from the spot where the assault was first committed. John Smith and William Edwards were called as witnesses. They corroborated the complainant's evidence as to the violence of the defendant's conduct, but the former only deposed to the first assault having been committed by one of the defendants. His evidence was not very clear on this point.

The defendant, Edw. Batcock, when called upon for his defence, said that he was accosted in the manner described by the complainant, but did not strike him before the complainant had first struck him no less than three times; after he had struck him twice he had told him "I will take but one more." No sooner was the word spoken than he received the third. He admitted having then returned the blows, when the complainant was assisted by seven or eight other persons who beat and kicked him while on the ground, and the other defendant who lived a little distant from the spot having been sent for by his mother, came to his assistance.

Mrs. Maria Badcock (*sic*), the mother, corroborated this statement. The Magistrates, after deliberating, convicted the defendants in the penalty of 25s. including costs, and ordered them to find sureties to keep the peace for twelve months. The required sureties were found.

28.12.1844.

MANSLAUGHTER

SWANSEA PETTY SESSIONS. – At these sessions, held at the Townhall, on Tuesday, before the Revs. Dr. Howard and J. Collins, T. Edw. Thomas and W. Ireland, Jones, Esqrs., Christopher Batcock, miller of Llanrhidian, appeared before the Bench, charged with most seriously having assaulted an old man named William Eynon, toll-collector at the Cadisford gate, at the extremity of Fairwood Common.

From the statement of the Rev. J. Collins, it appeared that on Sunday last, he was requested as a magistrate, to visit Eynon's house. On arriving there he found Eynon in a state of insensibility, produced, according to his wife's allegation, by the defendant's violence. Thinking Eynon's life to be in jeopardy, he reduced to writing the wife's evidence, and issued a warrant for the apprehension of Batcock, who was subsequently liberated on giving bail for his appearance – From the wife's depositions which were read by Mr. Collins, it appeared that late on Saturday night, she (Mrs. Eynon) and her husband were aroused by loud cries of "gate, gate," upon which her husband went out. She then heard him speak to parties outside – heard him telling them, "why should you want the gate opened, as you have no horse. You can walk through the side rails." Repeated demands to have the gate opened were subsequently made, upon which she proceeded to the door and saw two persons near the gate, one being the prisoner. The other she did not know. The two men passed through the gate, and proceeded a little distance – high words taking place between them and Eynon, who had followed them. She then observed the prisoner take up a stone, with which he violently struck her husband, inflicting a most severe wound on the bridge of the nose. Her husband immediately fell to the road in a state of insensibility, and remained there until she with the assistance of some neighbours, conveyed him to the house and placed him on a bed. The part of the road on which he stood was covered with blood. He had not given utterance to a single sentence up to that day. Mr. Perry, surgeon, was then sent for, and after examining Eynon pronounced him to be in a most dangerous state. – Mr. Perry, on being examined by the magistrates, stated that Eynon was still lying in a very dangerous state. It was a question upon which considerable doubt existed in his (Mr. Perry's) mind, whether he would eventually recover. He feared that the chances were against him. – The Magistrates intimated that the prisoner must be remanded until the result of the injuries could be ascertained. – Batcock stated that he could produce persons who were ready to offer themselves as securities for his appearance whenever called upon. – The Magistrates informed him that the case was of a character which rendered it impossible for them legally to accept bail, the medical man having stated that Eynon's life was in danger. Under these circumstances directions to keep the prisoner in custody were given.

4.1.1845.
Spring Assizes
SERIOUS CASE OF MANSLAUGHTER. – It will be recollected, that in our last week's Petty Sessions report, mention was made of a charge preferred against Christopher Batcock, miller, of Llanrhidian, having seriously assaulted William Eynon, the toll-collector at the Cadisford Gate, Gower, by striking him violently with a stone on the head. Having heard the depositions of Eynon's wife, which had been taken down in writing by the Rev. John Collins, the Magistrates decided upon remanding Batcock (declining to accept bail for

his appearance), for the purpose of awaiting the result of the injuries sustained by the toll collector. We are very sorry to announce, that those injuries have terminated fatally, the unfortunate man (Eynon) having expired on Tuesday last. after remaining in a state of insensibility since the period of the occurrence. On Wednesday and (*sic*) inquest on the body was held before C. Collins, Esq. coroner, and a jury composed of the inhabitants of the neighbourhood, and was adjourned to Thursday. Mrs. Eynon's evidence was similar to that previously given, that late on the night of the 21st inst., she and her deceased husband were disturbed by loud cries of "Gate, gate." She beckoned the deceased, who was rather deaf, being about 70 years of age, to go and open the gate. He opened the door of the house, and went out. She then heard him disputing with some persons outside, to whom he said, "What do you want the gate opened for, you have no horses and can pass through the side rails." This was followed by louder and repeated demands by the parties that the gate should be opened. She (Mrs. Eynon) proceeded to the door and saw that the persons who had the altercation with her husband were Batcock, the prisoner, and another man whom she did not know. The two men and her husband had, by this time, gone a few paces lower down than the gate, and angry words took place between them. She then observed Batcock pick up a stone, which he threw with violence at her husband, who instantly fell senseless to the ground. She gave the alarm, and with the assistance of some of the neighbours, had the deceased conveyed to the house and placed on a bed. The spot of the road on which he lay was covered with blood. He was most assiduously attended by Mr. J. G. Perry, surgeon, until Tuesday last when he expired, having remained insensible from the time in question. Morgan Kneath, a neighbour, corroborated the wife's evidence as to the appearances on the road, and the state of the deceased, &c. –

Mr. J. G. Perry, who had made a post-mortem examination of the body, described the internal appearances as healthy, and gave it as his undoubted opinion, that death was caused by the injuries sustained. Other witnesses were examined as to minor details, and among them Edwards, the person who accompanied Batcock at the time of the occurrence. This witness gave his evidence in a very prevaricating and reluctant manner. The coroner recapitulated the evidence; after which the jury consulted, and returned a verdict of "Manslaughter against Christopher Batcock." who was whereupon committed to prison under the coroner's warrant.

8.3.1845.
MANSLAUGHTER IN GOWER. – Christopher Long Batcock was indicted for having, on the 21st December, feloniously killed and slayed one William Eynon, by giving him a mortal wound on the head with a stone.

Mr. Benson stated the case for the prosecution. These circumstances being fully appeared in our paper at the time of the prisoner's committal. It appeared from the evidence of Elizabeth Eynon that she was the widow of the deceased, William Eynon, toll-collector at Catisford Gate, Gower. Late on the night in question, deceased and herself were sitting in the toll-house, when she heard a cry of "Gate, Gate." Her husband went out after which she heard him say , "Why do you cry out gate? Can't you pass through the side-rails?" Another person said "Damn your eyes, open the gate." She then went out and saw prisoner and another man named George Edwards in the road. It was the former who said "Damn your eyes, open the gate." I saw him pick up a stone, with which he struck the deceased on the head. Deceased immediately fell, and bled profusely. He remained in a state of delirium until his death in about ten days afterwards.

Cross-examined:– Saw a marline spike, which was brought in two days afterwards. My husband used to keep that in the house. Could not well have taken it out of the house without my knowing it.

Morgan Kneath examined, said he saw the deceased fall on the night in question, but did not recognise the party who gave the blow. Carried him to the house. The two men did not assist, saw no stick near him on the road.

George Edwards examined:– Was with the prisoner on the night in question. After prisoner cried "Gate" deceased came out, and seeing no horses, he said he would not open it. We went both by the footway. Some angry words arose between prisoner and Eynon. The latter pushed prisoner to the slope of the road. When Batcock came to the road the deceased aimed at him with a stick. Some blows again took place with sticks, both had sticks. Eynon then returned to his house, but came again after us. I was a little further on the road than Batcock, when I saw him stoop down and immediately afterwards deceased fell.

Mr. J. J. Perry was next called, who described the nature of the wounds which in his opinion had caused his death.

Elizabeth Kneath stated that she had found a marline-spike on the road two days after the occurrence.

Mr. V. Williams briefly: addressed the jury. The facts were such that no doubt could be entertained that the prisoner had unfortunately been the cause of the death of the deceased. He would have pleaded guilty, only that he thought all the facts had better come out, as there were some extenuating circumstances connected therewith.

Verdict, Guilty. – Sentence deferred.

SENTENCES – John Harries and Christopher Long Batcock were then placed at the bar for sentence.

His Lordship observed that they had been severally convicted of manslaughter, each of them the cause of the death of a fellow creature by an unlawful act; but there was a wide distinction between the two cases, for in the one (Harries's) a deadly instrument had been used, while in the other there was nothing to show that it was intended to cause any injuries as very serious as might cause death; still there were some circumstances of aggravation in the case, as the quarrel had been sought and commenced by the prisoner. With respect to Harries's case, it was one arising from the use of the knife, a crime dreadfully increased of late years in this and almost every other county. The prisoner not only used it once under the impulse of passion, but he had inflicted three separate wounds, each inflicted in a part of the body where it might prove fatal. After several additional observations, Harries was sentenced to transportation of Seven years: and Batcock to one year's imprisonment with hard labour.

CHARGE OF SHEEP STEALING
—Aug. 10th 1855—

This was a charge of some novelty and seriousness; the parties charged with the crime were well-known in the neighbourhood of Gower. The court was densely crowded during the whole time of hearing, several farmers from Gower and from Llanrhidian being present. Mr. J. R. Tripp appeared for the prosecution; Mr. J. R. Tripp for the defence.

Mr. Tripp briefly stated the case, observing that he appeared to support a charge against the two prisoners, Christopher Long Batcock and Francis Hancorne Batcock, for stealing three sheep, one the property of Mr. Wm. Thomas, and two the property of Mr. John Jenkins, both the prosecutors being farmers resident in Llanrhidian. Inasmuch as the evidence in both cases (with the exception of the identity of the sheep), would be precisely similar, he (Mr. Tripp), proposed to adopt a course to which there could be no legal objection, and which would save very much time, inasmuch as one statement of evidence would answer both charges. He thought it right to state thus early that although he purported to examine witnesses this day, from the peculiar nature of the case he would not be able to conclude the case this day. This being the fact, he had naturally considered whether it would be desirable to enter upon the case at all, but from various circumstances with which he was acquainted, he thought it would be desirable to examine the witnesses now in attendance. The case was one of a very peculiar nature, and therefore he preferred not to make any statement, and the more so, because he had only had but a very short opportunity of examining the witnesses, and therefore he might perhaps unintentionally state which could not be borne out by the evidence of the various witnesses which he should call before them. It was desirable therefore, that the Bench should hear the facts of the case from the witnesses themselves. Mr. Tripp then called George Harris, who, on being sworn and examined, said:– I am a labourer living in Llanrhidian. About one o'clock in the afternoon of Saturday last, I saw the prisoners, Christopher Long Badcock and Francis Hancorne Badcock, coming from Llanrhidian marsh with some sheep. They were going down towards the Higher Mill, in the parish of Llanrhidian, which is in the occupation of Christopher Long Badcock. The sheep went out of my sight, and I did not see them alive afterwards. The prisoners and the sheep were about 200 yards from the Higher Mill when I saw them. I was standing in a gateway, and the sheep passed close by me. I should say there were from twenty to thirty sheep before the prisoners. Some of these sheep I knew belong to the prisoners – the greatest part did – but some of the sheep belong to Mr. Jenkins, of Parkyrhedyn. I noticed some three or four of his sheep there – they had his mark upon them. One belonged to Wm. Thomas, the mason, of Llanrhidian – it had his mark upon it. I am at present, and have been for the last eleven years, in the service of Mr. Robert Davies, farmer. All the time I have been in his employ he has had sheep grazing on Llanrhidian marsh. He has had as many as 200 or 300 sheep on the marsh at one time. Most of my time during my service with Robert Davies, has been to look after my master's sheep on the marsh. In this way I have become acquainted with the several marks on the sheep which graze on the marsh. John Jenkins sheep has a round fork in the off ear, a spade under the near ear, and a round halfpenny also upon the near ear. Wm. Thomas's sheep are marked with a square fork on the near ear, and a spade on the off ear' and a "hack" under the spade on the edge of the ear. There was a pitch mark also on the rump, and on the near side. There was a "W" on the rump, and a "W" and a circle on the near side. I am certain that in the flock of sheep I saw before the prisoners, I saw one belonging to Wm. Thomas and three or four belonging to John Jenkins. A lamb got out of the flock, and the prisoners went to turn him back, whereupon I said "You might as well leave the lamb go back to the marsh." Francis Badcock said, "The mother of it was in the flock. I said, "No; the mother was not there."

He then asked me whose it was, and I told him it was Mr. Jenkins, of Parkyrhedyn. I then went to finish my dinner. Myself, Thomas Thomas and six other persons watched the prisoner's premises, the higher Mill, that night. We went to the mill about eleven o'clock.

After waiting about half and hour, I saw a light in the mill, and I then looked in through the works (the cog wheels of the water mill) of the mill. I saw both the prisoners in the mill. Christopher Badcock had a lighted candle in his hand. I saw Francis separate the leg from the loin of a quarter of mutton. I did not then see any other meat but the mutton.

Christopher Badcock marked with his finger a line showing how the mutton was to be cut. I continued to watch the mill until about half past one o'clock at night. During the whole of this time there was a light in the mill. About 12 o'clock the prisoner, Christopher, took down the carcass of a whole sheep which was hanging up on a pin in the mill, and threw it down on the bench where they used to cut up the meat I did not see them cut up this sheep. The prisoner Francis was also present when Christopher put the sheep on the bench. About ten minutes before left off watching, I saw both the prisoners by Christopher's door. Christopher had a bucket in his hand. I did not see anything in the garden. About eleven the same (Sunday) morning I assisted Jones in searching the river which runs from the Higher to the Lower Mill. I went into the river and picked up part of a sheep's ear. Mr. Jones and several other persons picked up several more pieces of a sheep's ear. I gave the pieces I picked up to P.S. Jones. The pieces were put together and one sheep's ear was formed. It was marked. I knew the mark; it was Wm. Thomas's mark. The river runs rapidly from the higher to the lower mill. Before we searched the river I went after Thomas Jones into a drying kiln belonging to Christopher Badcock, and adjoining the higher mill. In a wheelbarrow there, Thomas Jones found three sheepskins, 12 feet and a pair of shears. I examined the skins and observed that the legs and ears had been cut off the three skins – just such a cut as a butcher would in cutting off the feet. The three skins had the appearance of some of the wool having been cut off the sides of them. I found in the wheelbarrow some wool, with some pitch on it. The place where the wool had been cut off of two of the skins was the place where John Jenkins' pitch mark was. I know the sheep mark of the prisoners – they had no pitch marks on their sheep at all. The prisoner, Christopher Long Badcock, is a miller, and his brother. Francis Hancorn Badcock, is a joiner.

Cross-examined by Mr. Howard: The distance from the Higher Mill to the nearest end of Llanrhidian Marsh, is about a quarter of a mile. I did not see any of the sheep the prisoners were driving again alive. I did not look after the prisoners own sheep. I did not see either of the three alive again. I saw some of the prisoners' sheep on the marsh yesterday. It would take some five or ten minutes to drive from the Higher Mill to the marsh with a dog. I cannot tell how long without a dog. The sheep belonging to the prosecutor and also the prisoners, were small mountain sheep. I cannot separate my sheep from others on the marsh, without taking them in a place to do so. I have never known Badcock kill his own sheep on his premises. (Laughter.) There is a large pond by the higher mill. He has a good many men working at the pond lately. The prisoners sheared their lambs that day. I saw the lambs after they were sheared. I have never before seen a light in the mill at half past one o'clock in the morning. The wool found in the barrow, which had been cut off the sheep, was in small pieces. I could not form any letter out of the wool, neither could you. (Laughter.) The wool on mountain sheep is very short at this season of the year. I have known Mr. John Jenkins' sheep mark for the last eleven years; and the mark of Wm. Thomas for the same period. Both Mr. Jenkins and Mr. Thomas have many sheep on the marsh every year. Mr. Davies buys a good many sheep in the course of the year. Mr. Thomas buys and sells sheep some-times, and so does Mr. Jenkins.

Re-examined by Mr. Tripp:– The prisoners' sheep mark is a round fork in the off ear, and a "square halfpenny" under the near ear. [Skins produced] There were marks where the pitch had been cut off. [The sheep's ear picked up in the river was also produced]

Re-examination continued:– The mark on the of the ears now produced is the mark of Wm. Thomas; and the skin produced is also Mr. Thomas's.

Cross examined by Mr. Howard:– In order to get pitch off the skin I should put lime on it and then pluck the wool with my fingers. I should put lime on before I cut the pitch mark off. It is not usual to cut off the pitch mark before the wool is plucked off.

Thos. Gwyn, a weaver of Llanrhidian, sworn:– On Saturday night last, in consequence of some information I received, I agreed with Thos. Thomas and some other persons, to watch the Higher Mill, in occupation of Christopher Badcock and also the both prisoners' movements. About eleven o'clock that night I saw both the prisoners in the Dolphin public house where the prisoner Francis Hancorne Badcock and his mother live. We then went up together to the higher mill. We listened there, and found everything perfectly quiet. I then went to the house of the prosecutor, Wm. Thomas, and he joined myself and the others in watching the mill. After I returned from Wm. Thomas's, and returning to the higher mill, I went again to the Dolphin, and both the prisoners were still there. I then returned to Wm. Thomas and the others who had agreed to watch and we all then went up to near the mill. I was watching at about half past eleven o'clock, and the first thing I saw was a light in the mill, and I heard a noise as of chopping or pounding. I had not seen the prisoners anywhere from the time I saw them in the Dolphin, to the time I saw the light in the mill. I looked into the mill and then saw the two prisoners there. One of them (I think it was Francis) was cutting up mutton and the other was holding the candle. I saw two fore-quarters of a sheep in one piece. I afterwards saw the prisoner, Christopher take down the whole carcass of a sheep, which was hanging up in the mill. We continued watching up to about half past one, during which time we continued to look into the mill by turns. Sometime before we left off watching, I saw both the prisoners come out of the mill. They had something in their hands but I could not see what. They went towards the river where the waste water of the river comes out. I saw them return in about 20 minutes. I remained where I was. They both again entered the mill. I afterwards looked into the mill again and saw the two prisoners there, and the prisoner Christopher skinning a sheep's head, and Francis holding the candle. I afterwards saw Francis dividing the head with a saw. After I left off watching, I went to David Jones's house, and while there I saw the prisoners come out of the mill, and go into the drying kiln adjoining the mill. They both came out from the kiln, and entered the mill again. I again saw them leave the mill, and they then left in the direction of their houses.

Cross-examined by Mr. Howard. It was a bright moonlight night. I did not see the prisoners all the way down to the River. I watched them until a few yards of the river and they then turned round a corner out of my sight.

P.S. Thomas Jones, of the county constabulary, sworn: In consequence of information I received, I went to the house of the prisoner Christopher Long Badcock (*sic*), about half past eleven o'clock on Sunday morning last The other constable (Dav...) had arrived just before me. I saw both the prisoners there, I told them some sheep had been slaughtered in that neighbourhood the night before. There was then a leg of mutton hanging up in the room in which I found the prisoners; and (after pointing to the mutton), I asked them if there was any mutton in the house. Christopher replied "No". I asked him I (*sic*) should search the house, and he said, "I should". I then searched the room, and in another room, – in a bucket I found three sheeps' heads, and in the room saw the sheep's pluck; and in another bucket, a quantity of fat, and under the fat, five sheeps' kidneys. In a pantry (attached the room where I first saw the prisoners) I found another sheep's "pluck" with the heart and liver attached. I then asked the prisoners where the skins were, when the prisoner Christopher said, "They were up at the Dolphin," and said he would come and show them to me. He went outside of the house, but then said, "I will go myself, and you come up after me." I then took him back inside the house and handcuffed both prisoners. I then went from the house up to the drying kiln attached to the mill, where I found the three skins which I now produce, and two pairs of sheep shears. I found the wool with the pitch upon it in a wheelbarrow, I also found the 12 sheeps' feet, and two small sheeps' horns and two sheeps' tails, all of which I now produce. I also found a saw and an axe, with blood on them, in the mill which I afterwards searched. I then went back to Christopher's house again, and in the presence of the prisoners, I began to take up some bricks from the floor, having previously asked the prisoners where the meat was. First of all, Christopher said he would tell me where the meat was, but afterwards refused to do so, so it was then I began to take up the bricks. Christopher said, "You need not take up the bricks, for the meat is not there." I then went up to the mill, and in a carpenters shop over the mill (the door of which was locked) I found a pan, on a bench, containing six shoulders, five legs, six necks and attached to each other, and five(?) loins of mutton, the whole of which had been slightly sprinkled with salt. I then went and searched the river which runs from the higher to the lower mill. I was assisted by George Harris, Gwyn and others. Harris gave me one of the ears I now produce. I produce ten pieces of sheeps' ears, all of which was found either by myself, or others in my presence in the pond or the river. Some of the pieces were stitched together by P.C. Davies in my presence, forming a perfect ear, which I now produce. After searching the river, and on our way to Swansea, I told the prisoners I charged them with slaughtering three sheep, the property of William Thomas and John Jenkins, where upon the prisoner Christopher told me they had killed their own sheep.

Francis did not say a word.

Wm. Thomas, one of the prosecutors sworn and examined by Mr. Tripp:– I am a weaver. On Saturday last I had . . . sheep and four lambs on the Llanrhidian marsh. Out of this number ten were marked differently to the others; the ones I had purchased at the Neath Fair about ten months ago. Four were then marked thus – a top cut and a slit in the top cut of the near ear, and a spade on the off ear. The other six, a top cut and a slit in the off ear, and a spade under the near ear. These sheep remained unmarked with my own mark until about six or seven weeks ago, when I sheared them and then altered the ear mark to my own. I also place a mark on these to distinguish them from the other. I put a "W" on the rump, and a "W" in a circle on the side. I could not yesterday search the marsh for my sheep by reason of the severity of the weather. On Sunday morning last I went to Thomas Jones, the constable.

At this stage of the proceedings, the bench suggested an adjournment, inasmuch that it would impossible to complete the whole of the depositions that day. Both of the professional men coincided, and the case was accordingly adjourned until the following Thursday morning.

Mr. Tripp stated that, from circumstances that had recently come to his knowledge, it was his duty to ask the bench to bind over all the witnesses, in heavy recognizances (*sic*), to appear on that day.

Both prosecutors and the witnesses were then bound over in the sum of £40 each, to appear on Thursday to proceed with the charge. Mr. Tripp then applied and obtained a summons to compel the attendance of a very material witness, who had said he would not come forward unless compelled.

Mr. Howard said that both his clients were highly respectable, and were well known in the neighbourhood of Gower. They would give bail almost to any amount, he therefore applied to the bench to allow the prisoners to be out on bail until Thursday morning next.

The Magistrates: No, certainly not. We have considered that subject already.

The prisoners were then locked up.

10.9.1855.

THE SHEEP STEALING CASE.

Christopher Long Batcock, and Francis H. Batcock, two Gower farmers, remanded from Tuesday, charged with stealing three sheep, – two the property of Mr. Jenkins, and one of Mr. Wm. Thomas, both Gower farmers, were again brought up this day.

The prosecutor, Wm. Thomas was sworn, and in addition to the evidence given by him on Tuesday last, stated he called on P.S. Jones on Sunday last. The ten sheep which I purchased at Neath fair I saw on Sunday week last; they were then on the marsh. I have not since sold or disposed of neither of those sheep nor authorised any person so to do. I yesterday, with the assistance of several of my neighbours, searched the marshes (the higher and lower marsh) at Llanrhidian. We searched the marshes very carefully. We found nine only of the sheep: we could not find the tenth. We found 15 sheep on the marsh with the mark of Christopher Long Batcock – they are marked with lampblack by a 'streak' commencing on the middle of the back, going over the loin, and ending by the hind leg on each side. Thomas Jones accompanied me to Llanrhidian on Sunday morning last and apprehended the prisoners in my presence. After a little conversation Christopher called me back as I was going out of the house and told me the meat was in his workshop. I was present when Jones found the three sheep skins and the heads. I have since carefully examined the skins. I have compared my pitch marker with the pitch mark on the skins where the wool hade been partially cut off. It corresponded with one of the skins. Judging from this I believe it to be the skin of one of my sheep. It was the skin of a sheep, not of a lamb. I examined the heads and from my experience I can say two sheep were one year old, and the third three-year-old. The sheep I bought in Neath fair were one year old sheep. I know John Jenkins sheep mark. The places where the wool had been cut off corresponded with the places where he puts his mark on his sheep. I have examined the pieces of sheeps' ears found in the river, and found one ear to bear my mark. I marked it myself. This had the mark which was on it when I bought the sheep at Neath, and also my own mark. I marked it myself, I have no doubt of its being the ear of one of my sheep. I watched the Higher Mill on Saturday night last and saw the two prisoners engaged in cutting up sheep in the mill.

Cross examined by Mr. Howard:– I had lost sheep off the marsh before this and never found them. (Skins of the sheep of Mr. Thomas produced.) The marker corresponds with the marks on the skins; the places where the wool has been cut off the skins is, however, a little larger than the markers. I do not know the skin now produced except by the comparisons of my markers with the marks on it. I have no other marks on the skin with the exception of the pitch mark. By the Bench: If I wanted to cut off the mark "W," I should naturally cut off a little more wool than the size of the "W."

Re-examined by Mr. Tripp: There were no sheep grazing on Llanrhidian marsh with my mark on the same places. There were some other sheep on the marsh marked on the same places, but not with my mark.

By Mr. Howard: I swear that the skin now produced is one of my sheep. You shall find not a single sheep on Llanrhidian marsh marked with a circle on the side and a mark on the rump also. I will swear that the mark cut off the skin was a circle, because the place where the wool has been cut off is round. I swear that the mark cut of the skin was a "W" and a circle, and no other shape. (The pieces of the ears found in the river, which had been carefully preserved in spirits of wine, were here produced). I will swear that two of the pieces of ear now produced belonged to my sheep – they are marked by my mark. I made these marks some six or seven weeks ago, when I shear the sheep.

By Mr. Tripp: The sheep's ear now also produced by Thomas Jones is marked with the mark of John Jenkins. Thomas Thomas, shoemaker of Llanrhidian, sworn: He deposed that he saw the two prisoners driving sheep towards the Higher Mill. In about ten minutes or a quarter of an hour afterwards I saw Francis Badcock driving three sheep from the mill towards the marsh. I took particular notice of these three sheep – one of them had the mark of Mrs. Thomas (*sic*), of Llanrhidian, the second that of William Thomas, and the third Samuel Jones, of Gleason.

Re-examined by Mr. Howard: I did not reckon how many sheep the prisoners were originally driving. The mark on William Thomas's sheep was "WT" on the rump. There was no other pitch mark on that sheep. George Harris, recalled: About six or seven weeks ago I assisted to shear 15 sheep belonging to Christopher Badcock: they were all marked with lampblack over the back and hind quarters. Yesterday I found the 15 sheep on the marsh which I had previously helped to shear for Christopher.

Re-examined by Mr. Howard: At the time we sheared these sheep I do not think the prisoner Christopher told me some of his sheep were missing.

Re-examined by Mr. Tripp: I never saw more than 15 sheep belonging to the the prisoner Christopher Badcock.

Mr. John Jenkins, the other prosecutor, was called and examined: I was requested to search the marsh and see if my sheep were right. I was not on the marsh yesterday. I did not know the number of my sheep. On Saturday last I expect I had some sheep grazing at Llanrhidian. I have not seen them for the last three weeks. I had sheep on the marsh for some time. My sheep were marked – ear mark and a pitch mark "J." on the near side. My ear mark was a fork in the off ear, a spade under the near ear and a halfpenny also on the near ear. The mark on the ear now resembles my mark; it is exactly like mine. I did not tell Mr. Tripp "I will not swear this is my mark: but I believe it is – I have no doubt of it." According to the best of my belief it is my mark. When I was asked by Jones to search the marsh for my sheep, I said I would do so but I did not know the number of my sheep. I did not go to the marsh. (The bench – Then you have broken your word, for you told us you would. The witness gave his evidence with considerable reluctance.

Cross-examined by Mr. Howard : I did not reckon my sheep when I last sheared them, and therefore I cannot tell the number. I don't know I been in the marsh since. The mark in the ear produced is a "fork." It is an off ear. I have seen many sheep besides mine marked in the same way – it is a very common mark in a sheep's ear. I have seen several of my neighbours' sheep marked with the same mark. (Skins produced.) It looks very much like mine – there is a "redding" mark in some places. If there was a "J." on the near side, where the wool has been cut away, I could swear to it. I should put my mark just about the place where the wool has been cut off on the skin now produced. Now the wool has been cut off, I cannot say the skin is mine. I do not know what mark cut from that place. By the Bench: When I kill sheep I never take shears and cut the mark out before I sell the skins.

Examination by Mr. Howard continued: I cannot say that the second skin produced is mine. My sheep had "redding" marks on the rump. I think there is a redding mark on the skin produced. There is nothing I can swear to on the skin.

Re-examined by Mr. Tripp: My sheep, in addition to the ear mark had a mark of "J" on the near side and a redding mark on the rump. I never saw a sheep on Llanrhidian marsh marked with all three of my marks, unless that sheep was my property. I saw the two skins now produced by Thomas Jones on Sunday last. There was a redding mark on the rump of one – I did not notice it on the other. If the letter "J." was on the skins produced where the wool has been cut off I could then swear that the skins were mine.

This concluded the case for the prosecution.

Mr. Howard stated that as he had no opportunity of preparing any defence, he should advise his clients not to make any observations now, and he, on their behalf, should reserve any defence for a future occasion.

The price of the sheep was said to be 10s. each.

George Harris wished to make one correction in the evidence given by him on the first occasion. He had sworn that the ear produced and sewn together was the sheep of William Thomas: it was that of John Jenkins. (This mistake, it is only right to say, was rectified the moment the evidence was read over to him.)

The both prisoners were then fully committed to the next Quarter Sessions to take their trial for sheep stealing – the prosecutors being bound over in the sum of £100 each, and the witnesses in the sum of £50 each to prosecute.

Mr. Howard now applied that responsible bail be taken, and intimated that in the event of a refusal, he should possibly apply to one of her Majesty's Judges of the superior courts for such an indulgence. The Bench at once refused to accept bail, and stated that if an application was made to the Judge of a superior court, they (the magistrates) would no doubt be applied to for their reasons why they refused so to do, and they would then be quite ready and willing to give their reasons.

19.10.55.
CHARGE OF SHEEP STEALING

Christopher Long Batcock and Francis Hancorne Batcock, both of whom were stated to be able to read and write well, were charged with stealing one sheep, valued 10s., the property of Wm. Thomas, at Llanrhidian, on the 4th of August 1855.

Also, stealing two other sheep, valued 10s. each, the property of John Jenkins, of Llanrhidian, on the same day.

Counsel for the prosecution, Mr. Giffard, attorney, Mr. J. R. Tripp: Counsel for the defence, Mr. Henry Allen, attorney, Mr. J. Howard. The facts of the case are already well known to our readers. On the 4th day of August last, the elder prisoner had in his possession 15 sheep; these both prisoners were observed to drive into their mill on the day in question, and in the flock were the three sheep belonging to the prosecutor, and which they were now charged with stealing. From some suspicious circumstances, a strict watch of the mill belonging to the prisoners was kept, and in the dead of night a light was observed therein and both prisoners were found busily engaged in slaughtering some sheep. P.S. Jones of the county constabulary (to whom great praise is due for getting up the case) searched the house the next day, and, secreted in various parts, he found three sheep's heads, three sheep's skins and other portions of the sheep. The ears were picked up in a brook running under the mill. The skins and ears were produced at the trial and clearly identified as belonging to the sheep of the prosecutors. It was also proved that the prisoners flock still consisted of fifteen sheep after these three had been slaughtered. The jury instantly returned a verdict of guilty, and the Chairman, in giving the sentence of the court, observed that the prisoners seemed to have carried on one of the most systematic cases of sheep stealing he had ever remembered to have heard.

Sentenced to two years' imprisonment – the first two days in each month to be solitary confinement.

CHICKEN STEALING
11.5.60.
THE CASE OF BATCOCK

Christopher Long Batcock, a man of about 50 years of age, was brought up on remand on two separate cases of stealing fowls. Mr. Simons of Merthyr, appeared for the prisoner. – Mr. Henry Willis, miller, of Stackpool Mill, Reynoldstone, said that he resided with his uncle. On the 20th April last he had a hen and seven chickens in an outhouse, when he went to feed them in the evening. Early next morning the hen and seven chickens were gone. On the following day the seven chickens were shown him by P.C. John Shore. He would swear they were the same chickens.

(The live chickens were produced in court.) These chickens are the same age and description as those lost. He could swear most positively to one, from a peculiar whiteness about the bill.

Cross examined by Mr. Simons: He would swear positively that six of the chickens which he lost had top knots. He did not know how many grey or black ones were amongst those he lost. The prisoner belongs to Llanrhidian Mill. His (witness's) uncle was also a miller.

Mr. Thomas Willis of Stackpool Mill, Reynoldstone, also identified the chickens produced as those stolen from his outhouse, and which belonged to his nephew, the last witness.

Cross-examined by Mr. Simons: He could not say how many brown, or grey, or black chicken were in the brood. There was no peculiarity about the chickens by which he could identify them from others of a similar description. The door of the outhouse was kept closed: could not say that they had ever got out. Had not missed any fowls from foxes. Did not know that there were any foxes in the neighbourhood, except two-legged foxes. (Laughter.)

John Shore, P.C. No. 54, deposed that he searched the prisoner's house on the 27th day of April, by virtue of a search warrant under the hand and seal of Starling Benson, Esq. The first person he saw in the house was the prisoner's wife.

Prisoner was in bed in a downstairs room. He told prisoner he was charged with stealing two fowls from Samuel Jones, of Leason farm. Prisoner made no reply.

After he charged the prisoner, he saw Mrs. Batcock going upstairs rather hastily; he followed her and upstairs he found a basket containing five fowls, ready dressed for market. Mrs. Badcock threw a towel over the basket to hide them from view. He took the fowls into his possession. In a garden adjoining the mill he found the seven chickens which he now produced. They were running about the garden. He caught the chickens and took possession of them. Prisoner's wife laid hold of the heads of two of the chickens, and plucked the feathers out of their top-knots.

Mr. Simons contended that the acts of the wife could not be taken in evidence against the husband.

The Bench decided to have the fact recorded.

Witness said he asked Mr. (*sic*) Batcock why she pulled out the feathers of the chickens, and she said she was only stroking them down. When he took possession of the fowls, he asked prisoner where he got them from, but he made no reply. He then said, "They are Thos. Willis's chickens," to which prisoner said he could hatch chickens as well as Thomas Willis. He then took the prisoner into custody and conveyed him to Swansea. When on the road to Swansea, he and Samuel Jones, who accompanied him in the cart, got out (to) walk up a hill, when prisoner attempted to cut his throat. He (witness) turned round and saw prisoner bleeding, and asked him what was the matter. He said he had hurt himself. He was not in the habit of searching prisoners who were being conveyed to the station. The Mayor said he should always do so.

Superintendent Parsons said he always gave directions to his men to search persons who were charged with felony.

Examination continued: He found a knife in the prisoner's left hand waistcoat pocket (produced) – a long bladed weapon kept back by a spring when opened.

Cross-examined by Mr. Simons: The prisoner is deaf. On the previous night he searched the prisoner's cart, which he saw proceeding along the road; this was about one o'clock in the morning. The prisoner's nephew was then driving the cart.

By Mr. Davies: Mr. Hancorne attended the prisoner and stitched up the wound in his throat.

This being the evidence for the prosecution.

Mr. Simons contended that there was insufficient legal evidence to convict the prisoner. There was no evidence to show that the prisoner had himself stolen the property; the mere finding of stolen property on the premises of a prisoner, where other persons lived capable of committing the theft, was not sufficient to commit the prisoner for trial.

THE SECOND CHARGE

A second charge was preferred against the prisoner, of having stolen two fowls, the property of William Jones, of Leason, The prosecutor stated that he lived at Llanrhidian, and was a farmer. He resided with his father at Leason Farm. On the 26th April he saw the prisoner on his father's premises, about eleven o'clock at night. Watched him, and saw him go on to the farm, and return in about ten minutes from the field. Subsequently saw the prisoner, in company with another man, with a cart near Leason. Concealed himself opposite the cow-house at Leason Farm, and saw the prisoner and the other man walk up the road. Just as they passed the cow-house door a cock crew. The other man said, "There's fowls in there," and Batcock said, "Where?" The other man pointed to the cow-house door. Batcock said, "Let us go in," and they both went into the cow-house. In about half a minute he heard the fowls cry and make a noise with their wings. In about three minutes, saw both the men come out of the cow-house, with fowls in their hands, and crossed the fields towards Llanrhidian. He found two fow(l)s missing, and marks of blood which he traced on the way the prisoner and the other man took.

Cross-examined: With regard to the other man, I had my suspicion who it was, and told the policeman. Some further evidence was adduced, and the prisoner was committed on this charge also.

13.7.1860.
STEALING FOWLS – Christopher Long Batcock, 45, miller, was indicted for stealing seven chickens, the property of John Willis, of Llanrhidian, on the 21st of April; there was also another indictment for stealing two hen fowls, the property of Samuel Jones at the same place, on the 26th April. Mr. T. Allen, instructed by Mr. T. Attwood, attorney, Swansea, prosecuted, and the prisoner was defended by Mr. Lloyd, instructed by Mr. Morris, William Jones, son of the prosecutor, stated that he saw the prisoner and another man on the night in question; he watched them to his father's cow-house, where the fowls were. Whilst they were in he heard the fowls make a noise, and in a few minutes he saw them both come out with some fowls in their hands. When apprehended the prisoner did not deny the charge. Mr. Lloyd having addressed the jury for the prisoner, he was found guilty, and a former conviction for sheep stealing having been proved, he was sentenced to four years penal servitude.